The Work of All Ages

The Ongoing Plot to Rule the World
From Biblical Times to the Present

"[T]he Jews constitute but one percent of the human race. It suggests a nebulous dim puff of stardust lost in the blaze of the Milky Way. Properly, the Jew ought hardly to be heard of, but he is heard of, has always been heard of. He is as prominent on the planet as any other people, and his commercial importance is extravagantly out of proportion to the smallness of his bulk. . . ."

—MARK TWAIN
"Concerning The Jews"
Harper's Magazine, 1899

The Work of All Ages

The Ongoing Plot to Rule the World
From Biblical Times to the Present

By Peter Christian

Published by The Barnes Review

November 2010

The Work of All Ages
The Ongoing Plot to Rule the World From Biblical Times to the Present

By Peter Christian

Published by:
 THE BARNES REVIEW
 P.O. Box 15877
 Washington, D.C. 20003

 ISBN# 978-0-9846312-0-9

Ordering more copies:
Order more copies of *The WORK OF ALL AGES* (softcover, 230 pages, $25 plus $5 S&H) from The Barnes Review, P.O. Box 15877, Washington, D.C. 20003. TBR subscribers may take 10% off the list price. Call 1-877-773-9077 toll free to charge copies to Visa, MasterCard, AmEx or Discover. See more books and videos online at www.barnesreview.com.

Subscriptions:
A subscription to The Barnes Review historical magazine is $46 for one year (six issues) and $78 for two years (12 issues) inside the U.S. Outside the U.S: Canada/Mexico: $65 per year. All other nations: $80 per year sent via air mail. Send payment with request to TBR, P.O. Box 15877, Washington, D.C. 20003. Call 1-877-773-9077 toll free to charge to major credit cards. Order online at www.barnesreview.com. See a special subscription offer at the back of this volume or call toll free number above and ask for best current subscription offer.

Reproduction Policy:
Portions of this publication may be reproduced without prior permission in critical reviews and other papers if credit is given to author, book title is listed and full contact information and subscription information are given for publisher as shown above.

Table of Contents

Introduction: Who Controls America? 7
Chapter 1: Genesis 11
Chapter 2: Exodus 19
Chapter 3: The Conquest of Canaan 27
Chapter 4: Decline and Fall 37
Chapter 5: Christianity Rises 43
Chapter 6: The Roman Empire 51
Chapter 7: The Talmud 55
Chapter 8: The Rise of Islam 61
Chapter 9: The Khazars 65
Chapter 10: The Crusades 69
Chapter 11: The Late Middle Ages 77
Chapter 12: The Protestant Reformation 83
Chapter 13: Freemasonry 89
Chapter 14: The Rothschilds 93
Chapter 15: The Order of Illuminati 99
Chapter 16: Kabbalah 103
Chapter 17: The Sabbateans 109
Chapter 18: The Enlightenment 113
Chapter 19: The Pale of Settlement 119
Chapter 20: Communism 123
Chapter 21: Zionism 129
Chapter 22: The Protocols 133
Chapter 23: The Federal Reserve System 147
Chapter 24: The Russian Revolution 155
Chapter 25: The Holocaust 159
Chapter 26: The State of Israel 165
Chapter 27: Gaining Control of American Culture 173
Chapter 28: The Media 181
Chapter 29: Attacks on the Vatican 185
Chapter 30: Espionage 193
Chapter 31: The Police State 203
Chapter 32: Jewish Organizations 213
Chapter 33: International Organizations 219
Conclusion: At the Crossroad 225

INTRODUCTION

Who Controls America?

The Jews rule America now, so at last their story can be told and their accomplishments can be set forth. As the former prime minister of Israel, Ariel Sharon, said to his people on October 3, 2001, "We, the Jewish people, control America and the Americans know it."

Now that they control the world's only superpower they believe that nothing can defeat their ancient plan for world rule, as set forth in the Hebrew Bible. The Lord's promises to the Patriarchs and to Moses for a Jewish Messiah, who will lead the Israelites to rule of the world, may soon be fulfilled.

They have been the victims of prejudice for many centuries, but this has only made them stronger and better organized.

In America, they control the White House, the Congress, Wall Street, the media, education and the national culture. America has become a Jewish nation in many respects, even though it is nominally predominantly Christian.

There are about 5.4 million Jews in America today, out of a total population of more than 300 million, which amounts to less than 2% of the total, yet they predominate in banking, finance, real estate, government, the courts, law, medicine, accounting, movies, television, newspapers, magazines, book publishing and all the other activities that influence public opinion.

They believe that they are intellectually superior to the *goyim*. It is fitting that they should rule us.

They believe that they are God's chosen people, destined to rule the world, with Jerusalem as their capital and Greater Israel as their nation-state, growing from its present boundaries to extend from the Nile to the Euphrates, as it was in King David's day. You may wonder how it is possible that 15 million Jews can rule the world, with its population of more than 6 billion. It is because they are intellectually superior, rich, powerful, cunning, deceptive and extremely well organized. If anyone says anything against their religion, against Israel, against Zionism, or against any Jewish individual or group, they instantly attack him or her as anti-Semitic in their controlled news media and they withdraw their financial support. To criticize them is to commit political suicide.

Money is the root of their power. For many centuries they have been the leading bankers. The Rothschild family keeps a low profile, but they sit at the pinnacle of world power. There are many other powerful Jewish banking families: Loeb, Seligman, Baring, Schiff, Sassoon and Warburg, to name just a few. They have gotten control of the central banks of the world and from this their countries' wealth and economies, by their ability to create money out of thin air. Their unlimited supply of money allows them to buy the governments of the world, as well as the major business firms and the news media.

I will now share with you how their alleged intellectual superiority was able to overcome the other peoples of the world, starting in ancient times.

Now that they control the world's only superpower, they believe that nothing can defeat their ancient plan for world rule, as set forth in the Hebrew Bible.

Garden of Eden by Raphael

CHAPTER 1

Genesis

The Book of Genesis is the first book of the Hebrew Bible, as well as the Christian Bible. It starts with the stories of creation, Adam and Eve, Cain, Abel and Seth and their descendants to Noah and the Great Flood. Then it tells of Abram, later called Abraham, to whom the Lord promised an everlasting kingdom if he and his people would obey the Lord's commandments. Let's start with a review of these promises.

Genesis 12:1-3 says "Now the Lord said to Abram, 'Go from your country and your kindred and your father's house to the land that I will show you. I will make of you a great nation and I will bless you and make your name great, so that you will be a blessing. I will bless those who bless you and the one who curses you I will curse; and in you all the families of the earth shall be blessed.'"

Terah, Abram's father, had previously moved his family from Ur, in Chaldea, near Babylon, to Haran, in what is now southeastern Turkey. As the Lord commanded, Abram moved to Canaan, taking his wife Sarai (later called Sarah) and his nephew Lot. They traveled to Shechem, Bethel, the Negeb desert and eventually to Egypt, where they prospered until returning to Canaan.

The Lord told Abram in a dream that his offspring would be aliens and slaves in a foreign land and would be oppressed for 400 years. This land, of course, was Egypt. But He also made a very important covenant with Abram, as set forth in Genesis

15:18-21: "On that day the Lord made a covenant with Abram, saying, 'To your descendants I give this land, from the river of Egypt to the great river, the river Euphrates, the land of the Kenites, the Kenizzites, the Kadomites, the Hittites, the Perizzites, the Rephaim, the Amorites, the Canaanites, the Girgashites and the Jebusites.'" This promise was not fulfilled for several centuries, until the days of King David.

In chapter 16, we learn that Sarai was barren and that Abram had a son by Sarai's Egyptian slave-girl, Hagar. The son was Ishmael, who was to become the ancestor of a large family and by some accounts the ancestor of the Arabs.

Genesis 17:1-22 expands on the covenant. "When Abram was ninety-nine years old, the Lord appeared to Abram and said to him, 'I am God Almighty; walk before me and be blameless. And I will make my covenant between me and you and will make you exceedingly numerous.' Then Abram fell on his face; and God said to him, 'As for me, this is my covenant with you: You shall be the ancestor of a multitude of nations. No longer shall your name be Abram, but your name shall be Abraham; for I have made you the ancestor of a multitude of nations. I will make you exceedingly fruitful; and I will make nations of you and kings shall come from you. I will establish my covenant between me and you and your offspring after you throughout their generations, for an everlasting covenant, to be God to you and to your offspring after you. And I will give to you and to your offspring after you, the land where you are now an alien, all the land of Canaan, for a perpetual holding; and I will be their God.' God said to Abraham, 'As for you, you shall keep my covenant, you and your offspring after you throughout their generations. This is my covenant, which you shall keep, between me and you and your offspring after you: Every male among you shall be circumcised. You shall circumcise the flesh of your foreskins and it shall be a sign of the covenant between me and you. Throughout your generations every male among you shall be circumcised when he is eight days old, including the slave born in your house and the one bought with your money from any foreigner who is not of your offspring. Both the slave born in your house and the one bought with your money must be circumcised. So shall my covenant be in your flesh an everlasting covenant. Any uncircumcised male who is not circumcised in the flesh of his foreskin shall be cut off from his people; he has broken my covenant.' God said to Abraham, 'As for Sarai your wife, you shall not call her Sarai, but Sarah shall be her name. I will bless her and moreover I will give you a son by her. I will bless her and she shall give rise to nations; kings of peoples shall come from her.' Then Abraham fell on his face and laughed and said to himself, 'Can a child be born to a man who is a hundred years old? Can Sarah, who is ninety years old, bear a child?' And Abraham said to God, 'O that Ishmael might live in your Sight!' God said, 'No, but your wife Sarah shall bear you a son and you shall name him Isaac. I will establish my covenant with him as an everlasting covenant for his offspring after him. As for Ishmael, I have heard you; I will bless him and make him fruitful and exceedingly numerous; he shall be the father of twelve princes and I will make him a great nation. But my covenant I will establish with Isaac, whom Sarah shall bear to you at this season next year.' And when he had finished talking with him, God went up from Abraham."

As the Lord promised, Sarah bore a son and he was named Isaac as the Lord had directed. Several years later, the Lord decided to test Abraham, telling him to sacrifice Isaac. Although Abraham was greatly disturbed by the Lord's command, he set out to do as he was told. At the last minute before Isaac was to be killed, an angel intervened. The Lord was pleased with Abraham. At Genesis 22:16-18, the Lord said, "Because you have done this and have not withheld your son, your only son [sic], I will indeed bless you and I will make your offspring as numerous as the stars of heaven and as the sand that is on the seashore. And your offspring shall possess the gate of their enemies and by your offspring shall all the nations of the earth gain blessing for themselves, because you have obeyed my voice."

In the fullness of time, Isaac grew up and married Rebekah. They had twin sons, Esau and Jacob. Esau was born first, but Jacob later bought Esau's birthright for a bowl of porridge. During a time of famine, Isaac went to Gerar, in the land of the Philistines, planning to go to Egypt. Genesis 26:2-5 says as follows: The Lord appeared to Isaac and said, "Do not go down to Egypt; settle in the land that I shall show you. Reside in this land as an alien and I will be with you and bless you, for to you and to your descendants I will give all these lands and I will fulfill the oath that I swore to your father Abraham. I will make your offspring as numerous as the stars of heaven and will give to your offspring all these lands; and all the nations of the earth shall gain blessing for themselves through your offspring, because Abraham obeyed my voice and kept my charge, my commandments, my statutes and my laws."

When Isaac was dying, Jacob tricked him into giving Jacob, rather than Esau, his blessing. Isaac told Jacob to go to Padanaram to marry one of the daughters of Laban, Jacob's uncle. Jacob wanted to marry Rachel, the younger daughter and agreed to work for Laban for seven years for her. Laban tricked Jacob and substituted the elder daughter, Leah, into the wedding. Jacob agreed to serve Laban for another seven years for Rachel and ultimately married her. Rachel was barren. Leah bore four sons initially: Reuben, Simeon, Levi and Judah. Rachel gave her maid Bilhah to Jacob and she bore Dan and Naphtali. Leah thought she was no longer able to bear children and gave her maid Zilpah to Jacob; she bore Gad and Asher. Leah then bore Issachar and Zebulun and a daughter, Dinah. The Lord then opened Rachel's womb and she bore Joseph and later Benjamin. Thus Jacob had a total of twelve sons, each of whom was destined to become the ancestor of one of the twelve tribes of Israel.

The Lord told Jacob to leave Padanaram and come to Bethel, in the land of Canaan. Genesis 35:9-12 states the following. "God appeared to Jacob again when he came from Padanaram and he blessed him. God said to him, 'Your name is Jacob; no longer shall you be called Jacob, but Israel shall be your name.' So he was called Israel. God said to him, 'I am God Almighty: be fruitful and multiply; a nation and a company of nations shall come from you and kings shall spring from you. The land that I gave to Abraham and Isaac I will give to you and I will give the land to your offspring after you.'"

Thus we see clear biblical evidence of God's repeated promises to Abraham and his descendants of their future possession of the land of Canaan. The rest of the Book of Genesis tells of Joseph's sale to an Ishmaelite caravan by his brother Judah for 20 pieces of silver, Joseph's rise to power in Egypt, his marriage to Asenath, who bore his sons Manasseh and Ephraim, his reconciliation to his brothers and his acquisition of wealth for Pharaoh at the expense of his subjects during the years of famine.

Chapter 47 tells of the cleverness of Joseph. There was a famine in Egypt. The Egyptians asked Joseph for food, which he had stored in the granaries in expectation of the famine. Joseph took their livestock in exchange for food. The next year, he bought their land in exchange for food and made them slaves. He gave them seed to grow food and required them to give Pharaoh 20% of the crops. The Jews work similar plans today as they gradually accumulate the wealth of the world for themselves.

The story of the Hebrews, as they were known in Egypt, continues in the Book of Exodus.

At this point, it should be pointed out that most present-day Jewish scholars regard the Book of Genesis and indeed the entire Torah (Genesis, Exodus, Leviticus, Numbers and Deuteronomy) to be a collection of folk stories which convey important theological messages, rather than historical or scientific facts.

Take, for example, the creation stories at the very beginning of the Book of Genesis. The first, known as the Priestly version, Genesis 1:1 to 2:3, tells of God's creation of the Earth out of a watery chaos in six days. The Earth was a flat disk covered by a hard dome known as the firmament, in which the sun, moon and stars moved. God created the living creatures in the waters, sky and dry land and finally mankind, male and female.

The second account, known as the Jahwist version, Genesis 2:4-24, says that God made the Earth and the heavens, created man (but not woman) from the dust of the earth and breathed life into him, planted the Garden of Eden for him to till, then created the animals and birds and finally created woman out of one of man's ribs.

With the benefit of many centuries of scientific discovery and research, today we have a very different impression of creation. Even so, the vast majority of people believe that God created the heavens and the Earth, albeit in a different fashion than set forth in the Bible.

Another example of doubtful accuracy is the story of the Great Flood, set forth in Chapters 6 through 9 of Genesis. We are told two versions of this story as well. God was angry with mankind and determined to kill them all with a world-wide flood, saving only Noah, his family and a pair (or was it seven pairs?) of each species of animal in an ark which Noah was to build to God's specifications, about 450 feet long. It rained for 40 days and nights. The whole Earth was under water, remained so for 150 days and gradually the water receded over the next 150 days.

To cover the entire Earth would require a depth of water of more than 29,000 feet, the height of Mount Everest. Even Mount Ararat, where the ark first landed, is nearly 13,000 feet high. Yet we know that if all the polar ice caps melted, if all the underground aquifers were brought to the surface and if all the water vapor were wrung from the air, the water would rise less than 500 feet. Also, what would the people and the animals eat for the 340 days of the voyage? How could so many animals fit in an ark the size of an average-sized modern freighter?

Once again we see a story which is highly improbable, but the story tells us symbolically of God's power and His desire that we obey his laws.

The message of the Book of Genesis is extremely important to the modern world. God himself made repeated promises to his Chosen People that they would be given the land of Canaan forever. This is the basis of their Zionist claims for the State of Israel and its eventual expansion from the Nile to the Euphrates. They are now planning World War III to bring this about and to complete their goal of world conquest.

Let us now resume the narrative as told in the Old Testament Book of Exodus.

Statue of Moses by Michelangelo

CHAPTER 2

Exodus

The Book of Exodus tells the story of the Hebrews' departure from Egypt and the start of their 40-year journey in the wilderness *en route* to the Promised Land of Canaan. No dates are given in the Bible, but scholars estimate that this journey may have taken place about 1290 to 1240 B.C. Like the Book of Genesis, the Book of Exodus is not generally understood to be a literal historical document, but rather a collection of folk tales with important theological messages.

In Chapter 1, we learn that the Hebrews had grown rapidly in numbers in the 400 or 430 years since Israel brought his family of 70 members to Goshen, so much so that the Hebrews were more numerous than the native Egyptians. The Pharaoh ordered midwives to kill all male babies born to Hebrew women.

In Chapter 2, we learn that Moses was born to a Levite family, the son of Amram and Jochebed, who also had Aaron and Miriam earlier. In a gamble to save the baby's life, he was placed in a small boat and set adrift on the Nile. He was found by Pharaoh's daughter, who raised him as her own. When Moses was an adult, he killed an Egyptian for beating a Hebrew and fled to Midian, where he married Zipporah and had a son, Gershom.

In Chapter 3, we learn that Moses tended the flocks of his father-in-law Jethro (previously identified as Reuel). He came to Mount Horeb, where he saw a burning bush which was not consumed. God appeared to him and told him to return to Egypt to demand the release of the Hebrews from bondage.

Chapters 4 through 12 tell of Moses' conversations with Pharaoh demanding the release of the Hebrews, Pharaoh's refusals, God's sending a series of ten plagues on Egypt and Pharaoh's reluctant consent.

The story tells of the Hebrews crossing the Red Sea, which the Lord opened for them so they could pass through and closing the sea on the Egyptians who were pursuing them in their chariots, killing all of the Egyptians. The story continues with the long trek through the wilderness, during which Moses went up to the top of Mount Horeb, spoke with God and received the Ten Commandments. These appear at Genesis 20:1-17 and also at Deuteronomy 5:6-21 in slightly different wording. While Moses was on the mountain for 40 days and nights, his brother Aaron and the people made a golden calf to worship. When Moses came down from the mountain, he was angered by the golden calf, which he regarded as his peoples' breaking the covenant with God. He smashed the two tablets containing the commandments. Later he returned to the mountain for another 40 days, where God engraved a second set of tablets. God also gave Moses detailed instructions for the making of a tabernacle to house the ark of the covenant, which the Hebrews were to take with them on their journeys.

The Book of Exodus is full of improbable circumstances, which lead many modern scholars to believe that it is a collection of folk tales, rather than historical fact. We are told that more than 600,000 men were involved. The Book of Numbers says the group consisted of 603,550 men, age 20 or over. Apparently women and children were not considered important enough to count. If we assume that there were as many women as men and that there were four children per couple, the number of people involved would have been more than 2,400,000. These supposedly came from Israel's family of 70 people some 400 years earlier.

The distance from the city of Ramses, where most of the Hebrews lived, to the center of Canaan, is about 125 miles. A pedestrian could walk that distance in a matter of days, yet the Hebrews took a roundabout route in the wilderness which lasted 40 years.

A glance at the map of Egypt shows that in order to cross the Red Sea, the group would have had to go south from Ramses along the west bank of the Gulf of Suez, to the Red Sea, a distance of about 250 miles. Then they would cross the Red Sea, which is about 100 miles wide, into Arabia and the land of Midian. From there they would go north on the east side of the Gulf of Aqaba, to the city of Aqaba and then west into the Sinai. The total trip would be more than 500 miles and they would still be well south of their destination, Canaan.

It is unclear where Mount Horeb, also called Mount Sinai, is. If it is in the land of Midian, it is in Arabia. Perhaps it is in the southern part of the Sinai desert at Jebel Musa, or maybe in the northern part of the Sinai, at Jebel Helal.

The Bible does not give us any dates for the exodus, nor does it name the Pharaoh who was involved. Furthermore, Egyptian records make no mention of Moses, nor of a mass migration from that country. Where did the Hebrews get the materials and tools to make the golden calf and later the tabernacle, in the middle of the desert? The daily feeding of the masses by manna from heaven and the striking of the rock to produce water, seem improbable. All things considered, the Book of Exodus is of doubtful value as history, but important in giving the Ten Commandments and emphasizing the importance of following God's laws.

Modern scholars speculate that the Hebrews did not cross the Red Sea, but rather the Reed Sea, or Sea of Reeds, in the Nile delta. From there they went south to Mount Horeb/Sinai near the southern tip of the Sinai Peninsula. After Moses met with God, they went north and settled in Kadesh-barnea in the Negev desert, which is about 100 miles south of Jerusalem. There they stayed for about 38 years before they resumed their migration to Canaan.

Another theory is that the majority of the Israelites had settled in Kadesh-barnea for centuries and only a handful made the exodus from Egypt.

The Exodus story continues in the books of Leviticus, Numbers and Deuteronomy. The conquest of Canaan begins in the Book of Joshua.

The Book of Leviticus is mostly about priestly matters and the Holiness Code. The Lord spoke to Moses on a number of occasions, giving additional rules to be obeyed by the people. Eventually there were 613 laws written in the Torah. In addition to these, there were many laws which the Levite priests believed that the Lord gave to Moses during his long stays on Mount Horeb, but which were not written down until the Talmud was written many centuries later and which were not shared with the common people.

The Book of Numbers continues the story of the travels in the wilderness. The Israelites sent scouting parties into the land of Canaan, which was already inhabited by several tribes. They also visited the land of the Philistines, on the Mediterranean coast, where they were terrified by the tall, powerful inhabitants. They decided to go up the east side of the Dead Sea and to cross into Canaan in Jericho. Their travel was opposed by several groups, including the Edomites, Canaanites, Amorites and Moabites. The Israelites defeated these opponents and moved to the north end of the Dead Sea.

The Book of Deuteronomy (Second Law) was written in Judea about 625 B.C. and was appended to the other four books of the Torah by the Redactors in the post-exilic period. It is set in the exodus period and starts with Moses giving the people instructions about proper behavior and respect for God's laws prior to crossing the Jordan into Canaan.

Of particular importance is Deuteronomy 7:1-6. "When the Lord your God brings you into the land that you are about to enter and occupy and he clears away the many nations before you—the Hittites, the Girgashites, the Amorites, the Canaanites, the Perizzites, the Hivites and the Jebusites, seven nations mightier and more numerous than you—and when the Lord your God gives them over to you and you defeat them, then you must utterly destroy them. Make no covenant with them and show them no mercy. Do not intermarry with them, giving your daughters to their sons or taking their daughters for your sons, for that would turn away your children from following me, to serve other gods. Then the anger of the Lord would be kindled against you and he would destroy you quickly. But this is how you must deal with them: break down their altars, smash their pillars, hew down their sacred poles and burn their idols with fire. For you are a people holy to the Lord your God; the Lord your God has chosen you out of all the peoples on Earth to be his people, his treasured possession."

Please note that this passage contains several important points. First, when fighting for the land promised to their forefathers in Canaan, it is not enough to defeat their soldiers in battle; they must totally annihilate the enemy. This is the law of *cherem*. They are applying this rule today in Palestine. Second, they may not intermarry with the enemy. Third, they must destroy all vestiges of the enemy's religion. Fourth, the Israelites are God's chosen people.

Deuteronomy 11:22-24 reads as follows: "If you diligently observe this entire commandment that I am commanding you, loving the Lord your God, walking in all his ways and holding fast to him, then the Lord will drive out all these nations before you and you will dispossess nations larger and mightier than yourselves. Every place on which you set foot shall be yours; your territory shall extend from the wilderness to the Lebanon and from the River, the River Euphrates, to the Western Sea."

Deuteronomy 20 sets forth the rules of holy war. In the case of lands outside of Canaan, the men must be killed, but the women, children, livestock and property may be taken as spoil. But different rules apply in Canaan. Verses 16-18 state the following: "But as for the towns of these peoples that the Lord your God is giving you as an inheritance, you must not let anything that breathes remain alive. You shall annihilate them—the Hittites and the Amorites, the Canaanites and the Perizzites, the Hivites and the Jebusites—just as the Lord your God has commanded, so that they may not teach you to do all the abhorrent things that they do for their gods and you thus sin against the Lord your God."

Moses continued his discourse to the people. He turned over leadership of the nation to Joshua and blessed the Israelites. Then he went up Mount Nebo and died.

The story of the Israelites continues in the Book of Joshua.

Deuteronomy 20 sets forth the rules of holy war. In the case of lands outside of Canaan, the men must be killed, but the women, children, livestock and property may be taken as spoil.

Jericho destroyed

CHAPTER 3

The Conquest of Canaan

Having reviewed some pertinent portions of the Torah, let us now turn our attention to the next major section of the Hebrew Bible, the historical books. These are Joshua, Judges, Ruth, Samuel, Kings, Chronicles, Ezra-Nehemiah and Esther. When the 70 scholars translated the Hebrew Bible into Greek, starting about 250 B.C., producing the Septuagint, the Book of Kings was divided into two books, 1 Kings and 2 Kings. The Book of Chronicles was also divided into 1 Chronicles and 2 Chronicles and Ezra-Nehemiah was likewise divided into two books.

Scholars also recognize a separate classification, the Deuteronomistic History, consisting of the books of Deuteronomy, Joshua, Judges, Samuel and Kings. The books of Chronicles, Ezra-Nehemiah and Esther are not included in this grouping because they were written in the post-exilic period, whereas the included books were written close to the time period which they describe.

In all of these historical books, the theological message is more important than historical fact. Nowhere in the Hebrew Bible is a year date mentioned. In the Book of Kings and the later books, the time of the reigns of the kings is related to the time of the reigns of other kings, e.g. in the fifth year of King X of Judah, King Y began his reign over Israel. Certain contradictions make it impossible to determine the years when some of the kings actually reigned.

The Jewish calendar has a very long history. The Jewish New Year, Rosh Hashanah, this year will fall on 1 Tishrei 5771, which corresponds to September 9, 2010 on the Christian calendar. Thus the Jewish calendar predates the Christian calendar by 3,761 years. It is unfortunate that the Jewish scribes failed to list specific dates to the events about which they wrote, because it raises questions as to their credibility as historical documents.

The Book of Joshua describes the conquest of Canaan as a relatively short period of time, during the life of Joshua himself. In reality, the conquest took many centuries. Indeed, Israel reached the height of its expansion in the reign of King David, who ruled about 1,000 to 961 B.C. Even in his reign, the land of the Philistines, which were on the coastal area near the modern Gaza Strip and the land of the Phoenicians, near modern Lebanon, were never under permanent Israelite control.

Canaan, later called Palestine and now Israel, is a relatively small geographic land, about the size of the state of Massachusetts. Prior to the conquest by the Israelites, it was occupied by seven small nations, each with its own king. The wars were begun by Joshua and continued during the theocracy of the Judges and the later kingdoms. The United Kingdom lasted for less than a century, 1020 to 922 B.C. The northern kingdom of Israel split from the southern kingdom, Judah, and was defeated by the Assyrians in 722 B.C. and its ten tribes scattered. The southern kingdom, Judah, fell to the Babylonians in 597 B.C. Except for a period of self-rule under the Hasmoneans, Canaan was ruled by foreign powers until the state of Israel was established in 1948.

Let us now continue the story of the Israelites as told in the Book of Joshua. The tale begins with the Israelites camped in Shittim, on the east side of the Jordan River, making preparations to cross the river into Canaan. Like the earlier books, this one

THE CONQUEST OF CANAAN

contains several amazing events. The first of these was the opening of the Jordan River, allowing the Israelites to cross on dry land, reminiscent of the crossing of the Red/Reed Sea in Egypt.

The first city they attacked was Jericho, which was near the river and about ten miles north of the Dead Sea. The Israelites besieged the city. They marched around it for six days. On the seventh day, they blew their trumpets while marching around the city and amazingly the city walls fell. The inhabitants and the livestock were slaughtered, saving only Rahab and her family, who had helped the Israelites.

A man named Achan took some religious articles, which displeased the Lord. This caused the defeat of the Israelites at their next battle at Ai. Joshua had Achan stoned and burned. The next attack on Ai was successful.

When the Israelites were camped at Gibeon, the Hivites proposed to make a treaty with them, posing as strangers from a distant land. A treaty was made. When Joshua found that they deceived him, he let them live, but made them hewers of wood and drawers of water.

Five kings formed an alliance—under the leadership of the Amorites—against the Israelites. Joshua prevailed against the larger force. God also sent large hailstones which killed even more of the enemy that the Israelite soldiers did. The five kings were killed. The cities of Makkedah, Libnah, Lachish, Gezer, Eglon, Hebron and Debir were destroyed.

King Jabin of Hazor formed a coalition of Canaanites, Hittites, Amorites, Perizzites, Jebusites and Hivites. They were a large army, equipped with chariots and horses. Once again the Israelites prevailed against a much larger force. They hamstrung the horses, burned the chariots and took the city of Hazor.

Chapter 12 tells of further victories on both sides of the Jordan River by the Israelites. Chapters 13 through 22 describe the division of the conquered territory among the twelve tribes. The tribe of Levi had become priests, were located among the other tribes and had no land of their own. The tribe of Joseph, who had died in Egypt, was given to the descendants of his sons, Manasseh and Ephraim, thereby restoring the number of tribes to twelve. The tribes of Reuben and Gad and half of the tribe of Manasseh, which had large flocks of livestock, were given territory east of the Jordan. The land west of the Jordan was not entirely under Israelite control until the days of King David and even then the lands of the Philistines and the Phoenicians, on the shore of the Mediterranean Sea, remained independent. The land controlled by the Israelites was allocated by lot.

Joshua called the people together at Sechem for a renewal of the covenant with God. He died at age 110.

Now we come to the Book of Judges. The Tribe of Judah led the fighting against the Canaanites, but were unable to drive the Jebusites out of Jerusalem. The Israelites began to worship other gods, especially Baal and Astarte. The Lord then raised up a number of judges to rule the people as a theocracy. Among these were Deborah, Gideon, Samson and Samuel, with the latter being the subject of the Book of Samuel.

Tales of amazing victories continue with Gideon. With an army of only 300 men, each equipped with a trumpet and a jar, he was able to defeat the Midianites, killing 120,000 of them.

Samson was raised as a Nazarite, but he did not keep his vows. He married a Philistine woman. He killed a lion barehanded. He fell in love with Delilah, who pried the secret of his strength from him and led to his ruin. Blinded, he was taken to the temple of Dagon, where he pushed the main pillars apart, causing the temple to collapse, killing supposedly thousands of Philistines, as well as himself.

The Book of Ruth is part of the festival scrolls in the Hebrew Bible, but it is inserted between the Books of Judges and Samuel in Christian bibles because it is set in the same time period. Ruth was a Moabite woman who married an Israelite man. When her husband died, she went from Moab with her mother-in-law, Naomi, to Bethlehem. There she married a wealthy man, Boaz. They had a son, Obed, who later became the father of Jesse and the grandfather of King David.

God is not mentioned in the Book of Ruth. The story of the conquest of Canaan resumes in the Book of Samuel, which is one book in the Hebrew Bible, but divided into two books in the Septuagint and thus in the Christian Bible. In the latter, 1 Samuel has three main sections: the stories of Samuel (Chapters 1-7), Saul (Chapters 8-15) and David (Chapters 16-31). 2 Samuel covers the period from David's becoming king through his son Solomon's reign.

Samuel was raised as a Nazarite, under the tutelage of the priest Eli at Shiloh. The Lord called Samuel to be a prophet and a judge.

The Philistines fought the Israelites and captured the ark of the covenant and took it to the temple of Dagon in Ashdod. On two successive nights, the statue of Dagon fell from its pedestal. The ark was then moved to Gath, where more troubles occurred and then to Ekron, where panic and tumors occurred. After seven months, the ark was returned to the Israelites with a guilt offering.

The elders asked Samuel to appoint a king to rule them. This was offensive to the Lord, because the Lord was the real ruler of the Israelites through the Judges.

After repeated entreaties, the Lord told Samuel to anoint Saul as King of Israel. Saul gathered an army to oppose the Ammonites, who were besieging Jabesh-gilead. Saul routed them. He was made king in Gilgal.

Saul then made war with the Philistines, who had assembled a large force at Michmash, including 30,000 chariots and 6,000 horsemen. With a force of 10,000, the Israelites were again victorious.

The Lord told Saul to attack the Amalekites, who had opposed the Israelites' journey from Egypt. The Amalekites were descendants of Amalek, a grandson of Esau and a traditional enemy. Saul defeated the Amalekites, but contrary to the Lord's orders, allowed King Agag to live and kept the livestock. The Lord was angry with Saul for not annihilating the enemy and decided to replace him as king. Samuel killed Agag.

The Lord sent Samuel to Jesse in Bethlehem to select a successor for King Saul. The Lord picked David, the youngest of Jesse's sons. Samuel anointed David as the future king.

Chapter 17 tells the famous story of David's killing the Philistine giant, Goliath, with his sling.

The story continues with the account of King Saul's jealousy of David and his attempts to kill the young man. On two occasions, David had a chance to kill Saul, but spared his life. Samuel died and was buried at Ramah. Saul eventually committed suicide after the Philistines killed his sons in battle. This takes us to the end of 1 Samuel and the beginning of 2 Samuel in the Christian Bible.

After Saul's death, David became King of Judah and was anointed at Hebron. War broke out between Judah and Israel. After ruling Judah for seven years, David became king of the combined kingdom for 33 years.

David captured Jerusalem from the Jebusites and made it the capital of the kingdom. David went on to become the most successful conqueror in the history of Israel. At its peak, his empire extended from the Sinai to well north of Damascus and included the lands of Edom, Moab and Ammon east of the Jordan River. His successor, King Solomon, had economic influence all the way to the Euphrates River. Thus his kingdom included all of modern Israel except the Gaza-to-Joppa land of the Philistines and parts of Egypt, Jordan, Lebanon and Syria.

This history is especially important today, because one of the

THE CONQUEST OF CANAAN

objectives of the Zionist movement is to expand the state of Israel to include all of this territory and to rule the world from Jerusalem. Certain Jews are planning World War III to bring this about.

King David was a great hero, but he was not without faults. He committed adultery with Bathsheba and arranged to have her husband, Uriah the Hittite, killed in battle. He was condemned by the prophet Nathan. Their first child died. Their second son, Solomon, eventually became his successor.

The story continues in the Book of Kings. As noted previously, this book was one of those which were divided into two parts in the Septuagint. In this chapter, we will do an overview of the spectacular reign of Solomon.

When King David was old, his son Adonijah prepared to succeed him, but Zadok and Nathan anointed Solomon.

Solomon prayed to the Lord for wisdom and discernment, which the Lord was glad to give him. The story of his decision about two women who were claiming to be the mother of a baby is well known. Some of the Book of Proverbs is attributed to him.

Solomon's reign was relatively peaceful. Many public works projects were undertaken, including the building of the Temple, which took seven years to build and a much larger palace, which took 13 years. The construction crew included 30,000 forced laborers, which led to resentment against the king.

The Lord appeared to Solomon, promising him a royal throne forever, as he had promised David, if he followed the laws of the Lord. But at 1 Kings 9:6-7 the Lord issued a warning which was to have great significance: "If you turn aside from following me, you and your children and do not keep my commandments and my statutes that I have set before you, but go and serve other gods and worship them, then I will cut Israel off from the land that I have given them; and the house that I have consecrated for my name I will cast out of my sight; and Israel will become a proverb and a taunt among all peoples."

We are told that Solomon had 700 foreign princesses and 300 concubines among his wives. Most likely this is not true. The writers of the scriptures are known for making gross exaggerations to make a point, as we have seen on several previous occasions.

With these foreign wives came sanctuaries for a number of foreign gods, including Astarte, Milcom, Chemosh and Molech. The Lord decided to take away the greater part of the kingdom from Solomon when he died, leaving only Judah and Benjamin for his son, Rehoboam. Jeroboam, an Ephraimite, was promised the northern part of the kingdom, with its ten tribes.

Solomon died in 922 B.C., having ruled for 40 years. His son Rehoboam succeeded him in Judah, but was rejected in the north (Israel).

The Book of Kings continues with the story of the divided kingdom. We will resume the narrative in the next chapter, Decline and Fall.

One of the objectives of the Zionist movement is to expand the State of Israel to include much of the Mideast and to rule the world from Jerusalem. Certain Jews are planning World War III to bring this about.

CHAPTER 4

Decline and Fall

The Book of Kings continues with the story of the divided kingdom. After the death of King Solomon, the northern tribes would not accept his son Rehoboam as king and instead made Jeroboam their king. Thus the united kingdom lasted less than 100 years, 1020-922 B.C. and split into two kingdoms: a northern kingdom called Israel with its capital at Sechem (later at Samaria) with ten tribes and a southern kingdom called Judah with its capital at Jerusalem with two tribes—Judah and Benjamin.

Israel quickly split from the Lord. Jeroboam set up temples in Bethel and Dan and houses in high places, staffed with priests who were not Levites. The prophet Ahijah told Jeroboam's wife that her husband had sinned against the Lord, that his kingdom would end without heirs and that Israel would be scattered beyond the Euphrates. The northern kingdom was to last only 200 years, when the Assyrians captured Samaria and scattered the people, starting the diaspora.

Most of the kings of Israel "did what was evil in the sight of the Lord," to quote a phrase repeated many times in the Book of Kings. The low point was reached in the reign of King Ahab, who ruled 869-850 and Queen Jezebel. The prophet Elijah predicted three years of drought, which came to pass.

Chapter 18 tells of Elijah challenging the prophets of Baal to a contest to see whether Baal or the Lord was more powerful. The

Lord won, of course and the prophets of Baal were put to death.
　　Shortly before the fall of Samaria in 722 B.C., the prophet Hosea delivered a crushing message to the nation of Israel, comparing it to an unfaithful wife. We read at Hosea 1:9 "... for you are not my people and I am not your God." Thus the covenants were broken. No longer could Israel count on the Lord's support. It is hard to imagine what effect this utter rejection had on the people. Most hoped for a reconciliation with the Lord, but others despaired and turned to other gods. Some even turned to Lucifer, the fallen angel, whom God had expelled from heaven for disobedience and who became God's principal enemy on Earth.

　　After the Assyrians captured Samaria, the people were scattered to various parts of the Assyrian Empire, which stretched from Egypt to Persia and to other places also. This was the first phase of the diaspora, which eventually spread Israelites over most of the world. Other peoples were brought in to populate the land. Only gradually did some Israelites return to their native land.

　　Meanwhile, the Kingdom of Judah was having its ups and downs. Some of the kings were very upright and most of the people were faithful to the Lord. The high point occurred during the reign of King Josiah, who ruled 640-609 B.C. A book of scripture was found in the Temple during repairs. This may have been the Book of Deuteronomy.

　　In any event, the book was read aloud to the people and King Josiah implemented many reforms.

　　After Josiah's reign, things went rapidly down hill in Judah, with four kings in quick succession. In 597 B.C., Jerusalem fell to the Babylonians and some of the leaders were taken to Babylon. A puppet king, Zedekiah, was installed, but in 587 he rebelled. Most of the remaining Judahites were taken to Babylon. Worst yet, the Temple was destroyed. It is hard to imagine how devastating this must have been to the people, especially in light of

DECLINE & FALL

Hosea's telling of the Lord's rejection of the Israelites and the capture of Samaria in 722. Thus began the Babylonian Exile, or Babylonian Captivity. During this period, the exiles were called Judahites, which was shortened to Jews. The exile lasted until 538, when King Cyrus of Persia, who had defeated the Babylonians, allowed the people to return to Judah. Not everyone took advantage of this opportunity, however. Most of Jerusalem had been destroyed, along with the Temple, whereas Babylon was a wealthy and cultured city. The Jews were an intelligent people and soon rose to positions of responsibility in Babylon and other places.

During the exile, the priests started to write down many of the scriptures, which had been passed down by word of mouth for many generations, in order to keep their faith alive. This effort continued for many years. The final wording of the Torah, as we know it today, is believed to have been put together by the priest Ezra by about 458 B.C.

The Book of Chronicles starts with a genealogy, beginning with Adam. It covers the descendants of Jacob/Israel in some detail, the period of the united kingdom and the kingdom of Judah. Little is said of the northern kingdom of Israel. In some instances, the story varies slightly from the corresponding accounts in the Book of Kings.

The Book of Ezra/Nehemiah covers the post-exilic period, starting with King Cyrus's edict in 538 which allowed the Israelites to return to their native land. Judah became the Persian province of Yehud. Reconstruction of the Temple and of Jerusalem progressed in stages. The Temple was finished in 515 B.C. A group led by Ezra reestablished the Torah as the authority for the Jews, completing the final version by about 458. A group led by Nehemiah led the restoration of Jerusalem and its walls and the repopulation of the city.

From this time forward, except for the Hasmonean period,

Judah was under the rule of foreign powers. Persia ruled from 538 to 332 B.C. Alexander the Great established the Macedonian Empire, introducing the Greek or Hellenistic period. This consisted of two sub-periods: the Ptolemaic/Egyptian period, 332-198 and the Seleucid/Syrian period, 198-168. The Jews revolted under the leadership of Judas Maccabeus and obtained self-rule for about a century, 166-63. Then the Roman legions under Pompey captured Jerusalem in 63 B.C. and Judea, as they renamed it, was under Roman rule until the Roman Empire collapsed in the 5th century A.D. By then the Jews had been expelled from Jerusalem.

Meanwhile, the Israelites in exile, starting in 722 B.C., continued to emphasize education and group solidarity. They spread far and wide. Some assimilated with the inhabitants of their new lands, but others kept their religious faith in spite of the many hardships. Because of their natural talents and hard work, they often advanced to positions of authority in their adopted countries. Many became skilled in banking, finance, tax collecting, foreign trade, commerce, law, medicine, intelligence and other professional fields. They kept in touch with each other and developed a truly international community which exists to this day.

Many became skilled in banking, finance, tax collecting, foreign trade, commerce, law, medicine, intelligence and other professional fields. They kept in touch with each other and developed an international community which exists to this day.

"THE RESURRECTION" BY MATTHIAS GRUNEWALD

CHAPTER 5

Christianity Rises

According to Christian lore, in about 7 B.C., a boy was born to a Jewish couple from Nazareth who happened to be in Bethlehem for a census. They named him Jesus. The family were descendants of King David, which is why they came to Bethlehem, the city where David was born. His biological father was not Joseph. His mother was Mary, a virgin whose egg was fertilized by the Holy Spirit, in accordance with angelic announcements to Joseph and Mary. Thus Jesus was the son of God, in Christian beliefs.

Naturally Jews have very different beliefs on this point, especially as set forth in the Talmud, to be discussed later.

King Herod was told that a future king was born in his land. He ordered his soldiers to kill all male babies under the age of two to eliminate possible competition for his throne. Joseph was warned of this in a dream and took his family to Egypt until King Herod died in 4 B.C. The family then returned to Nazareth, in Galilee.

The gospels tell of an event when Jesus was 12. After the Passover festival, he stayed in the Temple and had discussions with the priests, who were very impressed by his knowledge of the scriptures, even though he had little or no formal education.

Nothing is known of his life from age 12 to about 30, except that he was a carpenter, as was his father Joseph. At age 30 or so, he embarked on a ministry for about three years. It began with his baptism by his cousin John in the Jordan River, at which time the Lord declared that Jesus was his son, in whom he was well pleased.

Jesus then spent the next forty days and nights in the wilderness, where he fasted and was tempted by Satan three times, but rejected the temptations.

At this point he began recruiting twelve disciples, all men, who dropped what they were doing and traveled with him. In time, they came to call him rabbi. Later, he recruited seventy more disciples, including some women. Thus we have an entirely Jewish group, led by a Jew of Davidic ancestry and consisting entirely of Jewish followers.

Furthermore, in his sermon on the mount, after reciting the beatitudes, Jesus said, "Do not think that I have come to abolish the law of the prophets; I have come not to abolish but to fulfill. For truly I tell you, until heaven and earth pass away, not one letter, not one stroke of a letter, will pass from the law until all is accomplished."

However, in this same sermon he proceeded to express very different interpretations of a number of ancient laws. A few examples follow.

"You have heard that it was said to those of ancient times, 'You shall not murder; and 'whoever murders shall be liable to judgment.' But I say to you that if you are angry with a brother of sister, you will be liable to judgment."

"You have heard that it was said, 'You shall not commit adultery. But I say to you that everyone who looks at a woman with lust has already committed adultery with her in his heart."

"It was also said, 'Whoever divorces his wife, let him give her a certificate of divorce.' But I say to you that anyone who divorces his wife, except on the ground of unchastity, causes her to commit adultery; and whoever marries a divorced woman commits adultery."

"Again, you have heard that it was said to those of ancient times, 'You shall not swear falsely, but carry out the vows you have made to the Lord.' But I say to you, Do not swear at all."

"You have heard that it was said, 'An eye for an eye and a tooth for a tooth.' But I say to you, Do not resist an evildoer. But if anyone strikes you on the right cheek, turn the other also."

"You have heard that it was said, 'You shall love your neighbor and hate your enemy.' But I say to you, Love your enemies and pray for those who persecute you."

Thus Jesus preached a message of love and kindness which was substantially at variance with existing practices. The Pharisees, who were very pious and very obedient to the law, were particularly upset with Jesus' teachings. Jesus, in turn, was often critical of the Pharisees, referring to them at one point as the "synagogue of Satan." Sometimes he criticized the Sadducees, the civic and religious leaders, as well. Thus Jesus aroused the opposition of the Jewish leadership from the very beginning of his ministry.

The gospels tell of many instances of Jesus healing the sick and casting out demons. We are told of many miracles, including the feeding of the 5,000, calming the storm on the Sea of Galilee, walking on water, changing water into wine and raising Lazarus from the dead.

Another fantastic story is the Transfiguration. We are told that Jesus went up Mount Tabor in Galilee with his disciples Peter, James and John. Jesus' face shone like the sun and his clothes became as white as the light. Moses and Elijah appeared beside him. A bright cloud covered the mountaintop. The voice of the Lord came from the cloud, saying, "This is my son, the Beloved; listen to him."

Near the end of his ministry, he came to Jerusalem, where he went to the Temple and attacked the merchants and moneychangers, calling the Temple a "den of thieves."

That was the last straw for the Sanhedrin, which captured him with the help of his disciple Judas, tried him, convicted him of blasphemy and turned him over to the Roman governor, Pontius Pilate, for execution.

Pilate found no crime in Jesus and was inclined to release him. He offered to release either Jesus or another prisoner, Barabbas, a Zealot who had killed a Roman soldier. The crowd asked for the release of Barabbas and demanded the crucifixion of Jesus. Fearing a riot, Pilate ordered Jesus' execution.

One would expect Jesus' death to be the end of the story. However, according to Jesus' followers, Jesus rose from the dead on the third day and disappeared from his tomb, which was guarded by Roman soldiers. He was seen by many people and talked with them. Forty days later, he ascended to heaven.

The Jewish leaders wanted to stamp out this perceived heresy before it became widespread and searched for Jesus' disciples. According to the Book of Acts, fifty days after Jesus' resurrection from the dead, the Holy Spirit came to the disciples, gave them special powers and sent them on their ministry. They spread the word to Jew and Gentile alike.

Saul of Tarsus was a Pharisee. He set out to persecute the new Jewish sect known as the Nazarenes, which later became a new religion called Christianity. While on the road to Damascus to persecute that group, he had a vision of the risen Jesus which completely changed his life. He converted to the new religion and became its main apostle, even though he never met Jesus during his life on Earth and spoke Greek rather than Aramaic. He was later recognized as a saint by the Christian church and was called by his Greek name, Paul. To Jews, however, he was a traitor.

He wrote the first of the Christian scriptures, a series of letters to various churches which he had established or visited, which became known as the Epistles. His writings are a very important part of early Christian theology.

Jesus himself never wrote anything, as far as we know. When he spoke, he often spoke in parables, which of course are subject to many interpretations. He never intended to establish a new religion, but rather to re-define Judaism and to confirm the existing law.

His followers recognized him as the Messiah, long awaited by the Jews as their savior from oppression. One of the most fundamental differences between Jewish and Christian beliefs is the mission of the Messiah. The Jews believed that their Messiah would be a powerful person who would drive out their foreign rulers and establish an earthly kingdom ruled by Jews. Jesus, on the other hand, spoke of a heavenly, spiritual kingdom. He preached love of God and your neighbor, kindness, forgiveness, peace and similar ideas. He opposed violence and civil insurrection. Furthermore, ultimately he was crucified by the Romans. In no way did he fit the Jewish concept of a Messiah.

This difference remains important to this day. Zionism is a current political movement which has the goal of rule of the world from Jerusalem, not a heavenly kingdom after death.

The four canonical gospels—Matthew, Mark, Luke and John—were written about 35 to 65 years after Jesus' death, so they are not as historically accurate as contemporaneous writings would be. Their authors had differences of emphasis, hence there are many differences between them.

There are very few references to Jesus in pagan sources, other than in *The Annals* by Tacitus. Likewise, Jewish sources are few, other than the Jewish historian, Flavius Josephus. Thus the vast majority of the information which we have about Jesus comes from Christian sources, especially the four canonical gospels. It should be noted that there were many other gospels written—we now know of about 25—but they did not become part of the official canon.

Many Jews eventually became Christians, but antagonism between Jews and the converts grew rapidly. Jewish leaders tried to silence the apostles and to drive them out of Jerusalem. A question arose as to whether Gentiles had to become Jews before they could become Christians. Ultimately it was decided that they did not. Paul preached at Jewish synagogues, but was most successful in converting Gentiles to Christianity. Women had important places in the churches which Paul set up, whereas Judaism emphasized male leadership.

The Book of Hebrews added to the strain. Apparently it was a sermon delivered to a congregation of converts to Christianity by an unknown preacher. It maintained that Christianity is superior to Judaism. Jesus, being God's son, is superior to the prophets, to Moses and to the priests, all of whom are mortal men. Jesus is the high priest of a superior sanctuary—heaven, versus the Temple. Jesus is the fulfillment of the Jewish scriptures. Jesus brought a new covenant to replace the one broken with God by the Jews.

The final break occurred at the Council of Jamnia in A.D. 95, when the Jewish leadership declared that Christians could no longer worship in Jewish synagogues.

Shortly thereafter, the Talmud began to be written—one version in Palestine and a longer and more definitive version in Babylon. As we will see later, part of these works were extremely critical of Christianity. In time the Talmud became more important to Judaism than the Torah itself, especially among Orthodox Jews.

Much of the Talmud is very critical of Christianity. In time the Talmud became more important to Judaism than the Torah itself.

THE DESTRUCTION OF THE TEMPLE IN JERUSALEM

CHAPTER 6

The Roman Empire

As we saw earlier, the Roman legions under Pompey captured Jerusalem in 63 B.C. Judah was renamed Judea. The Hasmonean period of self-rule ended. Judea was to remain under Roman rule until A.D. 476, when the Roman Empire in the west ended.

Rome had been a republic for many years until Julius Caesar was assassinated in 44 B.C. A period of civil war followed. Augustus Caesar emerged as the first emperor in 27 B.C. He ruled until A.D. 14.

At its height, the Roman Empire completely surrounded the Mediterranean Sea, including all of North Africa. It included southern Britain, and extended east to Mesopotamia. It was able to enforce its laws and to suppress rebellions, a condition known as the *Pax Romana*. It built a vast network of roads. It had a common currency in use throughout the empire. Latin was the official language, but Koine, a dialect of Greek, was the most commonly used language in the East.

Romans worshiped a panoply of gods and goddesses, roughly equivalent to the Greek gods and goddesses. However, religious freedom was practiced most of the time. The monotheistic religions of Judaism and Christianity existed alongside the polytheistic religions, although there were periods of persecution. Ethics was considered to be a branch of philosophy, rather than of religion.

Few believed in an after-life. Instead, the objective was to secure the favor of the gods in order to have a pleasant life here and now. The gods were believed to be very close to man and very accessible. In fact, it was believed that man could become divine, especially if he happened to be the Roman emperor.

When the emperors claimed to be gods, Jews and Christians did not recognize their divinity and refused to bow down to them. This caused government persecutions in several periods. One of these was during the reign of Emperor Nero, who ordered the burning of a large section of Rome in A.D. 64 to allow for redevelopment and who blamed the fire on the Christians.

Jews have always had a rebellious element within their faith. From A.D. 67 to 73, there was a widespread Jewish revolt in Judea. During the course of the revolt, the second Temple was destroyed in A.D. 70. We do not know whether the Roman soldiers smashed the stone tablets containing the Ten Commandments, or whether they were somehow saved from destruction. In any event, the Temple was leveled. It is hard to imagine the psychological blow that was to Judaism. No longer was there a central place for worship and sacrifice, or a need for the Temple priesthood. The many synagogues scattered throughout the diaspora became the only places of worship. The powers of the Temple priests passed to the local rabbis. By about A.D. 200, the Talmud began to be written. We will look at this collection of writings later.

Another Jewish revolt broke out in A.D. 116-117. Still another, the Bar Kochba revolt, broke out in A.D. 132-135. Many Jews regarded Rabbi Bar Kochba as the Jewish Messiah and fought vigorously to oust Rome from Judea. The Roman army was much stronger than the Jews and easily won the war. However, Rome grew weary of the recurring revolts in this province. Jerusalem was destroyed. The inhabitants were scattered. Many were taken to Rome as slaves. It is amazing that this latest disaster did not spell the end of Judaism. Somehow the rabbis were able to keep their people together and the faith alive.

Meanwhile, Christianity spread throughout the Roman Empire. Christians were sometimes persecuted and were forced to worship secretly in small groups in order to avoid being fed to the lions in the Coliseum. Persecutions occurred in A.D. 250-251 during the reign of Emperor Decius, who demanded sacrifice to the Roman gods, which caused opposition by Jews and Christians alike. Another period of persecution came in A.D. 257-258 under Emperor Valerian, who issued edicts demanding loyalty to the emperor. In A.D. 303, Emperor Diocletian issued similar orders. Christians were again persecuted from 303 until A.D. 313 when Emperor Constantine issued the Edict of Toleration, putting an end to the persecution.

Emperor Diocletian, who ruled 284-305, found that the empire was increasingly difficult for one man to rule. He started the process of sub-dividing it into four parts at first, but ultimately into two parts: a western part, with its capital at Rome and an eastern part, with its capital at Byzantium.

Emperor Constantine ruled 306-337. In 312 he saw the sign of the cross before his battle against Maxentius at the Milvian Bridge and won the battle and with it, control of the western empire. He had the sign of the cross placed on his soldiers' shields. In 313, he issued the Edict of Toleration. In 330, he founded Constantinople as the New Rome, on the site of Byzantium. The eastern empire was called the Byzantine Empire and was to last more than 1,000 years until it fell to the Muslims in 1453. Constantine continued to worship the Roman gods, but he converted to Christianity on his deathbed.

The western Roman Empire gradually weakened and eventually fell to invaders from the north. The last emperor, Romulus Augustolus, ruled A.D. 475-467.

A Talmudic scholar

CHAPTER 7

The Talmud

Let us now turn our attention to the Talmud, a collection of Jewish writings that eventually surpassed even the Torah in importance to Orthodox Jews. It consisted originally of two main parts: the Mishna, the oral law and the Gemara, rabbinical commentaries on the Mishna.

When Moses was on Mount Sinai talking with the Lord for two periods of 40 days each, he was told many things which became the subject matter of the oral law and which the Levite priests felt were too complex for the average person to understand. They kept this part of the law to themselves and did not share it with the *am'haretz* (common people). The written law consisted of the Ten Commandments and 613 *mitzvot* which the Lord later communicated to Moses.

After the second Temple was destroyed by the Romans in A.D. 70, there was no longer a need for a temple priesthood. Rabbis took over religious leadership and the many synagogues became the only remaining places of worship.

It was feared that the oral law would soon be lost, so the rabbis began to write it down. The result was the Mishna. Rabbinical commentary on the Mishna followed, becoming the Gemara. There were two versions of the Gemara: one written in Palestine and the other in Babylon. The former became the Palestinian or Jerusalem version, completed about A.D. 400; the latter became the Babylonian version, completed about A.D. 500.

You may recall that Israelites from the Northern Kingdom had been scattered to the winds by the Assyrians in 722 B.C. Some of these exiles settled in Babylon. Later, in 587 B.C., the Babylonians exiled many Judeans to Babylon. King Cyrus allowed them to return to Judea in 538 B.C., but many chose to remain in Babylon. Thus Babylon had a substantial Jewish community by the time the Talmud was written. Furthermore, Babylon was part of the Persian Empire in A.D. 70, whereas Palestine was part of the Roman Empire. Zoroastrianism was the prevailing religion in Persia at this time. Jews supported the Persian rulers and opposed the Roman Empire. The Babylonian version of the Talmud was more extensive and more influential than the Palestinian version. It was also more anti-Gentile and especially more anti-Christian. Many Christians were martyred in Babylon.

A moment's reflection will show why this hate existed. The Israelites had a long history of relationships with Gentile nations, referred to in Hebrew as the *goyim* and much of it was very unpleasant. In Egypt, where they spent some 400 years, they were slaves most of the time, required to do heavy manual labor. When they moved to Canaan, they were resisted by several neighboring tribes and had to fight wars of annihilation with the tribes already occupying Canaan. The Assyrians captured Samaria in 722 B.C. and scattered the ten northern tribes, placing others in the land. The Babylonians conquered Jerusalem in 597 B.C., held the Judeans in exile from 587 to 538 and destroyed the first Temple. The Persians were relatively benevolent rulers, but they were displaced by the Greeks, who ruled Canaan from 322 to 168 B.C. Jews enjoyed a century of self-rule until the Romans captured Jerusalem in 63 B.C. In A.D. 70, the Romans destroyed the second Temple. In A.D. 135, they destroyed Jerusalem altogether and expelled or killed the citizens.

Thus it is easy to see why the Jews developed a profound hatred of the *goyim*. They are a people with a long memory and a de-

THE TALMUD

sire for revenge. They are not inclined to forgive and forget. The Christian teachings of love your neighbor and turn the other cheek are not part of their belief system.

Quite naturally, this hatred found its way into the writings of the rabbis in the Talmud, along with many other matters of faith and daily living. Over the centuries, the Talmud became a vast encyclopedia of teachings and an anti-Christian extension of the Torah.

One of the basic premises of the Talmud is that Jews are the superior race, while Gentiles are sub-human, little better than animals. Rabbi Shimon ben Yohai said, "Even the best of the Gentiles should be killed." If it is all right to kill Gentiles, then any manner of lesser offenses is permissible. The Talmud teaches that it is all right to cheat, rob, rape, lie to, or enslave Gentiles. Of course there are limits to this. Most Jews live in countries where crimes, especially murder, will bring punishment of the offenders, so such crimes are to be avoided unless one can get away with it.

Another basic premise is that one set of rules applies to activities within the Jewish community and another set of rules applies to Jewish relationships with Gentiles. For example, it is unlawful for Jews to charge interest or usury to other Jews, but it is not only permissible, but desirable, to do so to Gentiles.

Another fundamental rule is that rabbis are to be obeyed. Anyone who disobeys a rabbi deserves death and will suffer in hell.

The rabbis who wrote the Talmud, being descendants of the Levites and the Judean Pharisees, believed that even the ten lost tribes of Israel will have no share in the world to come.

Scattered throughout the Talmud are many passages which are critical of Christianity. Here are a few samples:

- Mary was a whore.
- Jesus was not born of a virgin, but was the son of a Roman soldier, Pantera.
- Jesus was not the son of God, nor was he the Messiah.

- The Jews of old were right to condemn Jesus as a blasphemer and idolator.
- Jesus got what he deserved when he was crucified.
- Jesus is being punished in hell forever, immersed in boiling excrement.
- His followers will suffer the same fate.
- Jesus was not a descendant of King David.
- Jesus learned witchcraft while in Egypt.
- The whole story of the gospels is a fraud.
- Jesus had an affair with Mary Magdalene.
- Jesus practiced magic and deceived Israel.
- Jesus was stoned and hanged by the Jews, not killed by the Romans.
- Jesus' body was stolen from the tomb.
- His followers claimed that he rose from the dead.
- The cross is an idolatrous image.
- It is permissible to spit on the cross, crucifix, a church, or a Christian.

The Talmud contains hundreds of rules on many subjects, including many rules affecting daily life. For example, it is not lawful to travel more than 2,000 cubits (about 3,000 feet) on the Sabbath. Thus one must live within that distance of his synagogue.

Jewish women must not study the Talmud, but this is the highest activity for men. Details of personal and sexual life are regulated in great detail.

In the Jewish world today, Orthodox Jews regard the Talmud as superior to the Torah, even to the extent that the opinions of the rabbis sometimes overrule the word of God. Reform congregations reject the Talmud and cling to the Torah. Conservative congregations accept part of both writings. In the United States today, where more than five million Jews live, there are congregations of all three types. In Israel, the Orthodox congregations

THE TALMUD

are by far the most prevalent.

In the past, great pains were taken to keep the contents of the Talmud from the Gentiles and especially the Christians. Jesus was given various names to conceal his true identity. Even so, the contents of the Talmud became known to their arch-enemy, the Roman Catholic Church. On a number of occasions, Talmudic writings were rounded up and burned by Church authorities. Even so, the Popes have consistently ruled that Jews are not to be forcibly converted to Christianity and they are not to be disturbed in their synagogues or worship.

In yeshivas today, study focuses on the Talmud, rather than the Torah. The Torah fits in one average-sized book, whereas the Talmud has become the size of an encyclopedia. The Torah is a collection of folk stories and was often edited and revised. The Talmud is based on the Torah and is the result of many centuries of Jewish thought and interpretation. The Torah presents the Israelites as fallible human beings who occasionally do things which are less than honorable. The Talmud is constantly being updated by way of current commentaries and thus it relates to the world today.

Ironically, a large portion of Jews today place little emphasis on the Torah, or any of the Hebrew Bible for that matter. On the other hand, the Hebrew Bible is incorporated in its entirety into the Christian Bible, where it is called the Old Testament and occupies twice the space as the New Testament does. Many Christians, particularly Fundamentalists, believe in the literal accuracy of the entire Bible. Thus present day Christians put more faith in the Torah than even the Jews themselves.

Whatever your views about Judaism and the Talmud, it is well to remember that Jews now control America and may soon control the whole world.

Muhammad preaching

CHAPTER 8

The Rise of Islam

In A.D. 570, Muhammad was born to a prosperous family in Mecca. He was very religious. He prayed every year during the month of Ramadan in a cave near the summit of Mount Hira. About 610, he experienced the divine presence one night. The angel Gabriel conveyed God's words to him and told him to recite. He could neither read nor write, so he dictated the words to scribes over a period of about 23 years. The writings were assembled into the Qu'ran or Koran some 20 years after his death.

Many centuries earlier, Abraham had come to Mecca with his son, Ishmael. They built a temple to the Lord around a meteorite, the first temple of monotheistic belief, called the Ka'bah. Their descendants became twelve kingdoms in Arabia and eventually the first Muslims.

In Muhammad's day, Arabia had a mixture of religions, including Judaism, Christianity and various indigenous religions. When he started preaching God's word in Mecca, he encountered a lot of opposition, even though the new religion of Islam was based on Judaism and Christianity and was described as an update of those faiths, correcting their errors. The patriarchs from Abraham on were recognized. Jesus was regarded as a prophet, but not God. Muhammad was the last of the prophets, according to Islamic beliefs. Many passages from the Koran sound like passages from the Bible.

In 620, Muhammad made a night journey to Jerusalem. At the site of the Temple, he was transported to the seventh heaven and was returned to Jerusalem. Later the Dome of the Rock was built on this sacred site. This place is of importance to Jews also. It is where Abraham prepared to sacrifice Isaac (Muslims believe it was Ishmael) and where the Temple of Solomon was built. Jerusalem is sacred to Christians as well.

Islam found it necessary to fight many battles in order to survive. The concept of a just war was part of the faith from the beginning. In 622, Muslims were forced to flee Mecca. They fled to Yathrib, later called Medina, about 250 miles to the north. The journey is called the *hijra* or hegira and marks the beginning of the Islamic calendar.

In 624, the Muslims defeated the Quraysh in the Battle of Badr, but were defeated the following year in the Battle of Uhuda. In 626, the Muslims expelled the Jewish tribe of al Nadir. In 627 came the War of the Ditch, where Meccans attacked the Muslims at Medina and were driven off. In 627, the Muslims raided the Jewish tribe of Quaryzah. The Treaty of Hudaybiyya recognized Muhammad's right to proselytize, but the Meccans broke the treaty. In 629 Muslims killed the Jews of Khaybar. Thus Muslim relations with Jews got off to a very bad start. In 630, the Muslims captured Mecca and converted the entire population to Islam. The Ka'bah was established as the religious center of Islam.

Muhammad died in 632. He had not designated a successor. His father-in-law, Abu Bakr, was made caliph, but several tribes refused to pay taxes. Wars of apostacy followed.

The Muslims continued their warlike ways and expanded their territory very rapidly, hoping to conquer the world. By 661, they had gained control of the rest of Arabia, made gains to the north in Syria, Iraq and Persia and had moved west into Egypt and North Africa as far as Tripoli.

The Omayyad Dynasty ruled 661-750. They attacked the Byzantine Empire, which was Christian, but Constantinople held. They went into Central Asia to the Indus River and further west in North Africa. From there they conquered part of the Iber-

THE RISE OF ISLAM

ian Peninsula in 711. Southern Spain was to remain in Muslim control until 1492. The Muslim march into Europe was finally stopped by the Frankish king, Charles Martel, in 732 at Poitiers and Tours.

The Abbasid Empire ruled 750-1258, with its capital at Baghdad. The caliphate was divided into a number of caliphates, emirates and kingdoms. An Omayyad emirate retained control of southern Spain, with its capital at Cordoba. A Fatimid caliphate ruled Egypt, 909-1171. Seljuk Turks came to power in Iraq and Persia in 1050. In later chapters we will consider the Crusades and the Mongol invasions and their effect on Islam and the world.

Let us now consider the main beliefs of the Islamic religion. Islam is one of the monotheistic faiths, believing in one God whom they call Allah, the all-powerful creator of the world. It continues in the traditions of Judaism and Christianity and like them, traces its roots to Abraham and his descendants. Muslims believe that errors had crept into the older faiths over the centuries and set about to correct them where necessary.

There are Five Pillars of the Islamic faith: reciting the creed. (There is no God but Allah. Mohammad is his Messenger); prayer five times daily and in the mosque on Fridays; almsgiving; fasting dawn to dusk during the month of Ramadan; hajj-pilgrimage to Mecca by all Muslims who are able.

The Koran is written in Arabic, which remains the official language of the faith though it has spread worldwide. The Koran and the hadiths—sayings of Muhammad—are the basic scriptures.

The question of the successor to Muhammad led to a major division in the faith. The majority of Muslims today are Sunni, but a large minority are Shia. The latter are the majority in Iran, a fact which will be discussed later. There are also a number of mystics, called Sufis. Sometimes there are wars between Islamic nations, such as the bitter Iraq-Iran war of 1980-1989. Jews use these differences to their advantage.

A Khazar warrior with victim

CHAPTER 9

The Khazars

The Khazars are a very important part of our story, because they are the ancestors of about 80% of the Jews in the world today. They are non-Semitic Jews because they never inhabited Canaan. Sometimes they are called the Thirteenth Tribe. They are the ancestors of the Ashkenazim, as distinguished from the Sephardim. They are also the ancestors of the Bolsheviks, who seized power in Russia in 1917.

The Khazars were a Mongol-Turkic tribe which originated about the 4th century A.D. They were nomads who lived in circular tents and moved throughout the Russian steppes. They were excellent horsemen; their cavalry won many battles with neighboring tribes.

At its height, Khazaria was a vast empire centered on the Caspian Sea, which was then known as the Khazarian Sea. The empire extended from the Black Sea to the Aral Sea and included much of what is today southwestern Russia and Khazakstan. They ruled the eastern and southern Slavs, the Volga Bulgars and the Kiev Rus, all of whom paid them tribute.

By the year A.D. 700, the Khazars controlled the Caucasus Mountains. The Byzantine Empire, which was Christian, was to their southwest. The Muslim Caliphate was to their southeast and was trying to expand northward into eastern Europe. Having a large army and having control of the Caucasus Mountains, the Khazars were able to stop the Muslim advance about the same time that Charles Martel stopped their advance in France. The Khazars fought the Muslims for more than a hundred years, until the Muslim drive was reduced by internal disputes.

The event of greatest importance to our study occurred about A.D. 740, although some sources place it as early as 679. The Khazars had a number of indigenous religions. They wondered about the power which was held by the Muslims, Christians and the Jews. Representatives of each of these faiths were invited to Khazaria to explain their religions. Khagan Bulan was the Great Khan of the Khazars in 740. He felt that the Jews made the most convincing presentation and converted to Judaism. Most of the imperial court did likewise. In time, Judaism became the official religion of the entire empire. We believe that it held Karaite views originally, a purist form of Judaism.

Bulan's successor, who took the Jewish name Obadiah, installed rabbinic Talmudic Judaism, which was the prevailing form of the faith at the time. He built synagogues and schools. This orientation prevails to this day.

In A.D. 800, Charlemagne, King of the Franks, became Holy Roman Emperor and thus the leader of Christian forces in western Europe.

The Rus were a Viking tribe who sailed along Europe's larger rivers in their longboats, plundering and conquering as they went. In 965, they defeated the Khazar overlords in Kiev, which today is in Ukraine. The Rus in time became the Russians and conquered a vast territory extending to the Pacific Ocean.

The Khazar empire fell into gradual decline, breaking up by the 13th century. The Khazars, now fully Jewish, migrated mostly westward into eastern Europe. Most moved to what is now the Crimea, Ukraine, Hungary, Germany, Poland, Lithuania and Russia. They became known as the Ashkenazim, or Eastern Jews, as distinguished from the Sephardim, who had originated in Canaan and spent many centuries in Spain.

As we will see later, in the 18th century, most of the Jews had settled in Poland, where they were given a considerable amount of self-rule. When Poland was partitioned, a large section of Poland became part of Russia and was known as the Pale of the Settlement. The Jews in that area became the bulk of the Bolsheviks in the Russian Revolution.

CHAPTER 10

The Crusades

In the period leading up to the Crusades, there were two events of relevance to our study. The first of these was the Great Schism, which occurred in 1054. The Roman Catholic church and the Eastern Orthodox churches formally split over theological and political differences, thereby dividing Christianity into two parts. The Byzantine Empire was at the center of the Eastern Orthodox church, with its Patriarch at Constantinople. That city, of course, was in the path between Europe and the Holy Land.

The other event was the invasion of England by the Duke of Normandy in 1066. The Normans were descendants of the Norwegian Vikings, who plundered coastal areas and rivers in their longboats. The Swedish branch of the Vikings became the Rus, who defeated the Jewish Khazars in Kiev in 965.

As we saw in Chapter 8, the Muslims conquered much of the area around the Mediterranean Sea. In 750, the Abbasids succeeded the Omayyad Dynasty. Their capital was Baghdad. They were tolerant of other religions. Christian pilgrims to the Holy Land were not molested.

Seljuk Turks rose to power in the Middle East in the 11th century. In 1055, they overthrew the Abbasid caliphate in Baghdad. They moved against the Christian Byzantine Empire in 1071, but were unable to defeat it. In 1085, they captured Jerusalem and started persecuting Christians.

In spite of the Great Schism, the Byzantine emperor, Alexis, appealed to the Pope for help against the Muslims. The recent Cluniac reforms had revitalized Christianity. Pilgrimages to the Holy Land became more frequent. Italian cities had been fighting the Muslims for centuries. The population of Europe was increasing, so there was a need for territorial expansion, particularly to offset the loss of territory to the Muslims over the last four centuries. Fellow Christians of the Byzantine Empire were threatened.

In 1095, Pope Urban II called the Council of Clermont. He urged the Christian rulers to stop fighting among themselves and to unite in a holy crusade against the Muslims. He promised spiritual and temporal rewards. Anyone who was killed in the wars was assured of a place in heaven. Land could be regained from the Muslims and allocated to the victors. There was a lot of booty to be had also.

In 1096, before the First Crusade could be assembled, a group of peasants, led by Peter the Hermit and Walter the Penniless, began their own crusade, called the People's Crusade or the Hermit's Crusade. They were a mob of about 40,000 people, totally unprepared for the task. Worse yet, they took it upon themselves to kill all the Jews they could find along the way. Some Jews found refuge in rulers' castles, but many were slaughtered. The mob was resisted at Constantinople and was annihilated by the Turks in Asia Minor.

The First Crusade (1096-1099) arrived in Constantinople in 1097, captured Antioch in 1098 and captured Jerusalem in 1099. Both Muslims and Jews were slaughtered. The Dome of the Rock was stripped. The Kingdom of Jerusalem was formed under Godfrey of Bouillon, who called himself Defender of the Holy Sepulcher. Since the crusades were sponsored by the Roman Catholic church, the Patriarch of Jerusalem had real power. The Priory of Zion was formed. They in turn formed the Knights Templar to defend pilgrims to the Holy Land. They later went on to become rich and powerful bankers. Knights Hospitaler were formed to run hospitals. They were also called Knights of St. John and still exist today doing charitable work. The Teutonic Knights were created soon after. Their work will be discussed shortly.

During the period of the Crusades, a secret order of Muslim religious fanatics was founded in Persia by Hasan al-Sabbah. They were called the Assassins because of their fondness for hashish. They were part of the Ismali branch of the Shiite sect. Their headquarters was a mountain stronghold in Alumut, which they captured in 1091. They developed a chain of hill forts in Persia and Syria from which they terrorized the Crusaders. They were defeated in Persia by the Mongols in 1256 and in Syria by the Mamelukes in 1272. Remnants of the group survive to this day in Syria, Iran, Oman, Zanzibar and India. The Agha Khan, a descendant of Ishmail, the seventh Shiite Imam, is their leader.

The Second Crusade (1147-1149) was called by Pope Eugenius III in 1145. The Muslims had captured Edessa in 1144. The Pope promised that those who served would have their debts to the Jews cancelled, a major blow to their wealth. St. Bernard of Clairvaux, a Cistercian abbot, persuaded Emperor Conrad III of the Holy Roman Empire and King Louis VII of France to lead the crusade. It was a complete failure. They were repelled at Damascus.

The Third Crusade (1187-1192) was called by Pope Gregory VIII. Saladin had united the Arabs from Baghdad to Cairo into a mighty force. They recaptured Jerusalem in 1187, then most of the rest of the Kingdom of Jerusalem. The Crusaders were led by King Richard the Lion-Hearted of England, King Philip of France and Emperor Frederick I Barbarossa of Germany. They captured Cyprus and recaptured Acre and Jaffa, but were unable to retake Jerusalem.

The Fourth Crusade (1202-1204) was called by Pope Innocent III. The Crusaders were mostly from France and Venice. Contrary to the wishes of the Pope, the main targets were rivals of Venice. They captured the seaport of Zara and then captured and sacked Constantinople. This served the commercial interests of Venice, but did nothing for the interests of Christianity against the Muslims.

The Children's Crusade (1212) was opposed by the Pope. It accomplished nothing. Children were lost, shipwrecked, or sold into slavery. They got only as far as Genoa and Marseilles, where they were captured by slave dealers.

The Fifth Crusade (1217-1221) was called by Pope Innocent III and the Fourth Lateran Council in 1215. Most of the crusaders were French. They intended to conquer Egypt for use as a base to attack Jerusalem. They captured Damietta, but surrendered it when they were stopped at Cairo.

While the Crusades were going on, a new threat emerged from the east—the Mongol invasions. Genghis Khan united the nomadic tribes in Mongolia and captured northern China in 1214. He then turned west toward Muslim territory near the Aral Sea. In 1219 he captured Bukhara and Samarkand, reached the Caspian Sea, crossed the Caucasus and moved north into Russia. In 1220 he conquered Afghanistan and Persia. In 1221 he battled Muslims at the Indus River. He then returned to Mongolia to put down the Tanguts rebellion. Other invasions were to follow.

The Sixth Crusade (1228-1229) was political rather than spiritual in purpose. It was led by Emperor Frederick II, who was excommunicated by the Pope. He was a good negotiator and persuaded the Muslims to name him King of Jerusalem.

In 1240, the Mongols returned and invaded central Europe. They captured and destroyed Kiev. In 1241, they moved into Poland, Hungary and Croatia. In 1242 they withdrew again temporarily. In 1243 they defeated the Seljuk Turkish state of Konya, thereby extending the Mongol Empire almost to the Mediterranean.

The Seventh Crusade (1248-1250) was led by King Louis IX of France. Once again Egypt was the target. The Crusaders were defeated. Louis was captured and held for a substantial ransom.

In 1258, the Mongols sacked Baghdad and ended the Muslim

THE CRUSADES

caliphate there. The White Horde ruled western Siberia. The Golden Horde ruled south Russia from Khazakhstan to the Volga River. They later became Muslims.

The Eighth Crusade (1270) was again led by King Louis IX of France, but this time it was directed against Tunis in North Africa. The King died there of pestilence.

From 1275 to 1295 Marco Polo, a Venetian, went to China. He met Kublai Khan in Peking. He was instrumental in re-establishing trade between Venice and China.

Acre fell to the Muslims in 1291, ending the Crusaders' campaign in the Holy Land. In retrospect, very little was accomplished and much blood was shed. Instead of driving out the Muslims, their position was strengthened. The Muslims resent this whole episode to this day. They call the United States, United Kingdom and Israel the Crusaders, as a pejorative term.

In addition to the above crusades to recapture the Holy Land from the Muslims, there were several other crusades worthy of mention here.

In 711, Moors (North African Muslims) crossed into the Iberian Peninsula and captured the southern part of what is now Spain and Portugal. Spanish crusades against them began in the 11th century and lasted until 1492, when the Spanish were victorious. The Muslims were expelled from Spain and so were the Jews who refused to convert to Christianity. We will discuss the fate of these Sephardic Jews in a later chapter.

The Albigensian Crusade (1209-1229) was directed at the Albigensians, also known as Cathars. It is said that they were destroyed by the Roman Catholic church because they were heretics who had a very holy lifestyle and simple, dualistic beliefs. The real reason for their destruction was that they were aware of the fact that Jesus married Mary Magdalene and had a daughter, Tamar, with her. After Jesus was crucified, Mary and her friends moved to southern France, near Albi and Provence. The family bloodline continued through the Merovingian kings to the present day. The crusade was run by the Cistercians. Provence was destroyed in 1229.

Another set of crusades was conducted by the Teutonic Knights over a period of about three centuries, 1229 to 1525. They fought for the Catholic cause against the Slavs of Prussia in 1229. Eventually they controlled the Baltic coast. In 1309 they seized Pomerania from Brandenburg. In 1410 they defeated the Poles at Tannenberg. In 1466 they lost West Prussia to Poland. In 1525, the order disbanded after their grand master, Albert of Brandenburg, accepted the Protestant Reformation.

Taken as a whole, the Middle Ages were characterized by almost continuous warfare. Yet if you think about it, the same could be said for any period of time. Ever since history began, there have been wars somewhere in the world. Once Jews reach their goal of world domination, they mean to make war impossible.

The Middle Ages were characterized by almost continuous warfare. The same could be said for any period of time. Ever since history began, there have been wars. Once Jews reach their goal of world domination, they mean to make war impossible.

Pope Innocent III

CHAPTER 11

The Late Middle Ages

In the last several chapters, we looked at events of the early Middle Ages, by which I mean the period after the fall of the Roman Empire in A.D. 476. We saw that the Babylonian Talmud was completed about A.D. 500 and gradually took on more importance that the Torah itself.

We traced the rise of Islam, which started about 610 and which spread rapidly throughout the Middle East, North Africa and Europe and we reviewed the conversion of the Khazars to Judaism about 740. This turned out to be an extremely important event, because about 80% of the Jews in the world today descended from this group, rather than from the Israelites.

We saw that the Great Schism, which formally divided the Roman Catholic Church form the Eastern Orthodox Churches, took place in 1054 and we reviewed the period of the Crusades, 1095 to 1291, when European armies tried unsuccessfully to drive the Muslims from the Holy Land, a campaign which is still resented by the Muslims to this day.

We noted the Albigensian Crusade, 1209 to 1229, directed at the Albigensians, also known as the Cathars, a Christian group whose ideas did not coincide with Roman Catholic orthodoxy.

Finally, we made note of the beginning of the Mongol invasions in 1219, which at their peak drove deeply into Europe.

Now let us briefly review several other developments that have had long-term significance.

In 1179 the Third Lateran Council made some rules for Christians regarding relations with Jews. There was to be no forced conversions to Christianity, no harm to their persons or goods and no disruptions to Jewish religious ceremonies. On the other hand, Jews were not to own Christian slaves, or to obtain control of Christian churches. These protections did not apply if Jews plotted to subvert the Christian faith. These rules were similar to the policies set centuries earlier by Pope Gregory the Great, who ruled 590-604.

In 1215, the Fourth Lateran Council enacted certain measures against Jews, who were required to wear distinctive clothing so Christians could avoid them.

In 1233, Pope Gregory IX set up the Holy Office of the Inquisition, primarily to stamp out the last remnants of the Albigensian heresy and also any other deviations from the official orthodoxy of the time.

Nicholas Dronin, a Jew, was expelled from the synagogue for his unorthodox views. He converted to Roman Catholicism. In 1236, he exposed the anti-Christian views of the Talmud to Pope Gregory IX. This defection put a major strain on Christian attitudes toward Judaism. The Pope ordered burning of the Talmud.

In 1290, King Edward I of England ordered all Jews to be expelled. This was the first of the wholesale expulsions of Jews from various cities, or entire countries, of Europe, most of which occurred in the 15th and 16th centuries. The reasons varied, but for the most part it was because the natural abilities and hard work of the Jews caused them to become wealthy, resulting in resentment among the Gentiles. This was particularly so when the Jews prospered by usury, or by tax farming.

In 1307, the Knights Templar were arrested on orders of King Philip IV of France. They were charged with heresy and acts of blasphemy, but the main reason was their extensive banking operations and accumulated wealth. The King owed them a lot of money. With the backing of Pope Clement V and the Grand Inquisitor of France, William of Paris, King Philip had all the Templars he could find arrested on Friday, October 13, 1307. That is why Friday the 13th is considered to be an unlucky day. Their property was transferred to the Knights of St. John. Jacques de Molay, the grand master, was one of the people arrested. He was burned at the stake in Paris on March 14, 1314. Those who escaped were expelled from France, as were the Jewish bankers. A number of the Templars went to Scotland.

In 1348 to 1350, the Black Death plague took many lives in Europe. Jews were blamed for it. This was completely unfair, of course, but false ideas can be believed.

In the 15th century, Jews were expelled from a number of European cities, or even entire countries. In 1421, they were expelled from Vienna and Linz, 1424 from Cologne, 1435 from Speyer, 1438 from Mainz, 1483 from Seville, 1492 from Italy and the rest of Spain and 1496 from Portugal.

The expulsion from Spain was particularly painful. Some Jews had been in Spain since the Assyrian conquest in 722 B.C. and became known as Sephardic Jews. They had become very wealthy from their monopoly on usury, while most Christians were poor. This caused a lot of resentment against the Jews. In 1394, rioting broke out in Seville and spread to other cities. Some Jews were killed and synagogues were demolished. In 1413, Jews were required to defend the Talmud in the Disputation of Tortora. In the 15th century, they were ordered to convert to Christianity or leave the country. Many did convert—the Conversos, as they were called—although some continued to practice their Jewish faith secretly. Vincent Ferrer converted many by his preaching. In 1478, Pope Sixtus IV set up the Spanish Inquisition, which became notorious for its brutality. Converts who continued to practice Judaism were the main targets. Many of them were tortured and killed. In 1492, Spain under Ferdinand and Isabella conquered the Moors in southern Spain and drove them out of the country. Jews were expelled as well. The Jews settled all over Europe, especially in Amsterdam and Antwerp, where they established thriving commercial centers.

Also in the 15th century, Jewish ideas began to infiltrate the Roman Catholic Church. Pico della Mirandola introduced neo-Platonism and Kabbalah to Pope Sixtus IV. The Kabbalah was translated into Latin. Mysticism was by no means confined to Judaism. Christianity had many mystics, especially in the Middle Ages and Islam had its Sufi mystics. In Chapter 16, we will discuss Kabbalah and the other mystic beliefs.

In 1453, Constantinople fell to the Ottoman Turks, ending the Byzantine Empire which had begun in the 4th century. The Ottoman Empire was to have a long life also, continuing until World War I. The loss of Constantinople was a major disaster for Christianity, but it had some positive results. Many of the inhabitants emigrated to Europe, bringing their developed culture with them. They made a major contribution to the Renaissance, the rebirth of culture and civilization in Europe.

In 1517, Johannes Reuchlin wrote *On the Art of Kabbalah* and dedicated it to Pope Leo X.

In 1540, the Society of Jesus, better known as Jesuits, was formed by Ignatius Loyola. It strongly opposed the revolutionary movement.

In 1542, The Holy Office of the Inquisition resumed its work, this time against the Protestant Reformation, an effort known as the Roman Inquisition. We will explore this subject in the next chapter.

In 1558, the Book of Zohar was published. This was the most important single book in Kabbalah.

In 1564, the Council of Trent allowed the publication of the Talmud, provided that the anti-Christian passages were deleted.

In 1579, Rosicrucianism was founded by Johann Andrea. It

was a reorganization of the Knights Templar. Its members included Jews. The Kabbalah was part of its belief system, along with Greek philosophy, Gnosticism and Hermeticism. In later years it became the basis of Freemasonry and the Royal Society.

> *The Third Lateran Council made some rules for Christians regarding relations with Jews. There was to be no forced conversions to Christianity, no harm to their persons or goods and no disruptions to Jewish religious ceremonies.*

John Calvin

CHAPTER 12

The Protestant Reformation

The Protestant Reformation is usually thought to begin in 1517, when Martin Luther posted his famous 95 Theses. However, there were earlier events which are worthy of mention.

Jews have always considered Christianity to be their enemy and the Roman Catholic Church their anti-Semitic arch-enemy. Accordingly, whenever groups arose to oppose the church, Jews supported them. An enemy of our enemy is our friend. The creation of the Society of Jesus in 1540 increased Jewish opposition.

An early Protestant activity was the Hussite revolution, which broke out in Prague, Bohemia (now the Czech Republic) in 1415 and lasted until 1434. Its leader was John Huss, who was a friend of John Wycliffe. Both were opposed to ecclesiastics and favored the simple ideals of the early church. Bohemia was linked with Spain in the slave trade since antiquity and Jews were part of it. Jews had also developed an extensive commercial and intelligence network in Europe and beyond. Huss was supported by Waldensians, as well as by Jews.

In 1415, Huss was condemned by the Council of Constance and burned at the stake, but the movement went on. The Hussites set up headquarters in the mountains near Prague. One of them was renamed Mount Tabor, after the mountain in Galilee where

Jesus was transfigured. They considered themselves to be the modern Israelites and God's chosen people. They believed that the millennium was at hand and established an early form of communism with no private property. Tabor was a theocracy.

In 1418, Pope Martin V ordered a crusade against the Hussites. They proved to be a formidable opponent. They were not defeated until 1434.

The Protestant Reformation grew in earnest after 1517, when Martin Luther wrote his 95 Theses to promote reform of the Roman Catholic Church. He was a monk with somewhat humanistic views. He believed in the importance of the scriptures—only the scriptures. In 1520, he was excommunicated and declared a heretic by Pope Leo X. In 1521 Emperor Charles V issued the Edict of Worms, prohibiting Luther from expressing his views publicly. In 1525 he married a former nun.

Luther was a prolific writer. He translated the Bible into German, thereby making it available to many who did not understand Latin, Greek, or Hebrew. The New Testament appeared in 1522 and the complete Bible in 1534.

Philipp Melanchton had been one of his teachers and later became his principal follower. Thomas Muentzer was a friend and a revolutionary who later split with Luther.

Early in his career, Luther defended Jewish liberties to undermine the Roman Catholic Church. He hoped Jews would convert to Christianity. Jews supported the Reform cause. They printed translations of the Bible which the Church considered to be erroneous. Later in life, Luther became very anti-Jewish and urged the destruction of their synagogues and the burning of their books.

In 1530, Philipp Melanchthon wrote the Augsburg Confession, the set of beliefs which became the basis of the Lutheran Church. Lutheranism became a middle ground in Protestant thought, between the more conservative position of the Church of England and the more radical groups such as the Anabaptists.

Thomas Muentzer was a Roman Catholic priest and a revolutionary. Originally a friend of Martin Luther, they parted ways. In his sermons in Zwickau, he attacked the Pope, bishops, monks and scholasticism. He set off a revolution and was banned from the pulpit.

In 1521, he was expelled from Zwickau and went to Prague, where he was welcomed as a follower of John Huss. He formed the League of the Elect. In 1523, he moved to Allstedt as pastor of the Church of St. John. He created the first German-language liturgy.

In 1525, the Peasant Revolt broke out in Germany and spread to France and Italy. The peasants were defeated by Hessian troops. 100,000 peasants were killed. Muentzer was captured, tortured and killed.

Another Protestant group was the Anabaptists. They started in Switzerland in 1525 and spread quickly all over Europe. The leaders were Bernard Rothman, Jan Bokelzoon and Jan Matthys. They saw a sign in the sky—a bent arm holding a sword, with bloody hands in the clouds. In 1529, they began a revolution.

In 1533, they took over the city of Muenster, in Westphalia (now Germany) and set up a theocratic government. They called it the New Jerusalem and expected Jesus to return there soon. The Diet of Koblenz decided to put down the revolt and besieged the city. Many Anabaptists were killed, but some survived and fled to Bohemia and Moravia.

Anabaptist ideas survive to this day, although in non-violent forms such as the Mennonites, Amish, Baptists and Quakers.

Calvinism started in Switzerland under the leadership of John Calvin (1509-1564). It became the avant-garde of the revolutionary movement, opposed to Rome, Catholic Spain and the Inquisition. It had considerable support from like-minded Jews.

In 1541, the Calvinists established a police state in Geneva, with the help of a Jewish intelligence ring. John Calvin died in 1564, but the movement continued without him.

The Reformation spread to England, but for political rather than theological reasons. King Henry VIII was married to Catherine of Aragon, with whom he had only one living child, Mary. He was concerned that if he did not have a male heir, a war of succession would erupt. He therefore asked the Pope to annul his marriage so that he could marry Anne Boleyn. The Pope refused to grant the annulment. King Henry, although he was a faithful Catholic who was once cited by the Pope as the Defender of the Faith for his criticism of Martin Luther, decided to sever relations with the Vatican and declare himself the head of the Church of England. This was accomplished by the Act of Supremacy in 1534.

King Henry then married Anne Boleyn and had a daughter, Elizabeth, by her. He then divorced Anne and married Jane Seymour, with whom he finally had a son, Edward.

The Church of England became Protestant and eventually cast off many of its Catholic trappings. This caused great distress among loyal Catholics. Battles and intrigues occurred for many years. Francis Walsingham became the chief of intelligence for the Crown. He had the very able assistance of a vast network of Jewish intelligence operatives who uncovered many Jesuit-led plots against Henry's successors.

In 1566, an Iconoclast Rebellion broke out in Antwerp. It consisted of English Protestants, German Anabaptists and Sephardic Jews who had been expelled from Spain. They objected to the many religious statues and icons used by the Catholics. Jews also worked with the Dutch Calvinists against the Catholics.

Calvinism later inspired the colonization of New England by English Puritans in 1620 and the Puritan Revolution in England under Oliver Cromwell in 1645.

Jews have always considered Christianity to be their enemy, and the Roman Catholic Church their anti-Semitic arch-enemy. Accordingly, whenever groups arose to oppose the church, Jews supported them. An enemy of our enemy is our friend.

A Masonic ritual features a statue of Baphomet

CHAPTER 13

Freemasonry

Most people think of Freemasonry as a primarily Christian organization and indeed the majority of its members are Christians. However, it was formed entirely by Jews to destroy Christianity from behind the scenes. As Dr. Isaac Wise said, "Masonry is a Jewish institution, whose history, degrees, charges, passwords and explanations are Jewish from beginning to end." Jews are included in its membership, but they keep their true purposes hidden.

The foundations of Freemasonry go back to ancient Egypt, where the ancient Hebrews were residents and slaves for some 400 years. The Egyptian Trinity of Isis, Osiris and Horus, with his all-seeing eye, are part of it. The circle with the dot in the center symbolizes the sun and also male and female. Luciferianism and Illuminism are basic beliefs. Blood oaths are part of the basic ritual. The Christian god, called by them Adonai, is considered evil and Lucifer is worshiped, although this is not explained to members until they reach the highest degrees. Dualism, or good versus evil, is a basic belief. Other ideas were drawn from the Zoroastrians, Gnostics and Manicheans.

Freemasonry is a universal religion, open to anyone who believes in a supreme being. Jews are welcome and many have joined. Jewish ideas, such as the Temple and its architect, Hiram Abif, are included in the lore. The Talmudic Kabbalah is an integral part of the beliefs.

Freemasonry is an outgrowth of Rosicrucianism, which was organized in 1579. Sir Francis Bacon, a Rosicrucian, was one of the founders of Freemasonry. Unlike that secret brotherhood,

Freemasonry is an open society, although members must take life-threatening blood oaths not to reveal its secrets.

Many years after the death of Jacques de Molay, the grand master of the Knights Templar, the Gnostic tradition was resurrected by the Freemasons as a messianic political movement based on Jewish rituals and symbolism.

Freemasonry uses a hierarchal structure, an elaborate spy system, and the use of wealth to gain power under the cover of science and philanthropy. It includes oaths of secrecy.

By 1650, Freemasonry was strong in Scotland. Some traced their history to the near-destruction of the Knights Templar in 1307, after which some of the survivors fled to Scotland.

The first American lodge was formed by Jews in Newport, Rhode Island, in 1658. It consisted of 15 Jews from Holland. They were associated with the Truro synagogue.

The official founding of the Grand Lodge in London occurred in 1717. It served as an adjunct to the Whig Party, opposed to the Tories. The Grand Orient Lodge in Paris was a rival group with more secretive ideas. The Masonic Constitution was written in 1723 by James Anderson, a Scottish Presbyterian minister.

In 1738, Pope Clement XII issued a papal bull condemning Freemasonry and ordering Roman Catholics not to get involved with it under penalty of excommunication. He stated that Jews and freethinkers turned the lodges into agencies of subversion. Freemasons promoted the ideas of the French Revolution—liberty, equality and fraternity—and the idea of a future heaven on Earth. Liberty became the excuse for license, sexual liberation and immorality, overturning Catholic morality. In 1751, Pope Benedict XIV issued a similar bull.

Even so, Freemasonry grew rapidly in the 18th century. It had about 50,000 members by 1750. In America, many of the founding fathers were Freemasons, including George Washington. Many American Presidents have been Freemasons. Harry Truman was a 33rd degree Mason.

The basic structure of Freemasonry is the Blue Lodge, which consists of three degrees. The first degree is Entered Apprentice Mason. The second is Fellow Craft Mason and the third is Master Mason. Most Freemasons stop at that level. For those who wish to go further, there are two avenues: the Scottish Rite, with 32 degrees and the York Rite with 13. In the Scottish Rite, the highest degree is Sublime Prince of the Royal Secret, whose members become Shriners—Ancient and Accepted Order of Nobles of the Mystic Shrine. There is also an invitation-only 33rd degree, Sovereign Grand Inspector General. In the York Rite, the highest degree is Order of Knights Templar, reflecting the historic origin of Freemasonry.

Freemasonry suffered a major reversal in America in 1826. A member, Captain William Morgan, divulged Masonic secrets publicly, contrary to the Masonic oath. He was ritually murdered. The resulting scandal caused many to drop out of the organization.

In 1871, Albert Pike, the head of Freemasonry in America and Giuseppe Mazzini, an Italian leader, developed a plan for world conquest by means of three world wars. The first was to place an Illuminati dictatorship in Russia. This was accomplished by the Bolshevik Revolution in 1917, during World War I. The second was for Russia to capture Europe, which happened in World War II. The third was for the Battle of Armageddon, with Muslims against Christians and Jews. This may occur shortly, using Iran as the pretext for nuclear war. Freemasonry is an integral part of the Jewish plan for a New World Order, which could result in Israel being the ruler of the world.

In 1872, Albert Pike wrote *Morals and Dogma*, which has become the bible of Freemasonry. Originally it was given only to 33rd degree Masons and later to a wider audience. It set forth the beliefs of Freemasonry and identifies Lucifer, the Light Bearer, as the Masonic god.

Another Masonic leader, Manly Hall, wrote *The Secret Teachings of All Ages* in 1928.

A Rothschild uses vultures to pull a money chest

CHAPTER 14

The Rothschilds

One of the most brilliant men of all time was Mayer Amschel Bauer (1743-1812). He started his career as a goldsmith, silversmith and coin dealer. His shop in Frankfurt had a red shield as its outdoor sign, so he changed his name to Rothschild, German for red shield. He had ambitions to achieve great things.

In 1773, when he was only 30, he asked twelve wealthy and influential friends to join him for a meeting in his shop. His basic idea was for them to pool their resources in order to take control of the world by the use of money. He had studied the English civil war and learned from its mistakes. He planned to cause a revolution in France to advance his agenda. His friends agreed to his basic objective and he outlined the details to them.

He stated that men are inclined to do evil, rather than good, so they should be governed by violence and terrorism, rather than by reasoning. By the laws of nature, right lies in force. The law is the substitute for brute force.

He said that political freedom is an idea, not a fact. Control could be obtained by preaching liberalism to the electorate, persuading them to surrender a little of their power at a time.

The power of gold had already usurped the power of liberal rulers. The power of faith to rule had declined, replaced by freedom, leading to license. Capital is entirely in our hands, he told his friends.

Any means to reach the goal is justified. Rulers use cunning and deception. Frankness and honesty are vices in politics.

Our right lies in force. We can use force to reconstruct all existing institutions, he said.

To paraphrase: "The power of our resources must remain invisible until the very moment when it has gained such strength that no cunning or force can undermine it. Premature exposure would risk destroying the work of centuries.

"The ruler must use mob psychology. Absolute despotism is necessary to control the mindless mob.

"All forms of vice, including alcohol, drugs and moral corruption, must be used to corrupt the morals of youth. Bribery, deceit and treachery will serve our ends.

"The state has the right to seize property by any means if by doing so it secures submission and sovereignty.

"Liberty, equality and fraternity are terms we have used since ancient times to control the masses, but they have no place in nature. We have set up the aristocracy of money and wealth.

"We should foment wars to place governments in debt to us and to direct the peace process to our benefit.

"Public officials should be chosen from those who would be servile and obedient to our commands and pawns in our game.

"We must control all outlets of public information in order to spread our propaganda.

"Bad times must be blamed on others. We must appear to be the champions of the workers, even though our goal is the killing of the *goyim*.

"Industrial depressions and financial panics can be brought about to serve our purposes. We can create unemployment, hunger and shortages of food.

"We must infiltrate Freemasonry and set up Grand Orient Lodges of our own. We must carry out subversion under the cloak of philanthropy.

"We should use high-sounding phrases to mask our real intentions. Lavish promises can be made to the masses and the opposite done afterwards.

"We can use revolutionary war, street fighting and the reign of terror.

"After wars, secret diplomacy must be used to promote our ends without revealing our secret power behind the scenes.

"World government is the ultimate goal. Huge monopolies must be established to counter the largest fortunes of the *goyim*.

"Economic war must be waged to rob the *goyim* of their land and industries, using high taxes, unfair competition, control of raw materials and creation of labor unrest.

"The build-up of armaments should be encouraged so that the *goyim* should destroy each other in warfare.

"In the New World Order, members of the One World Government would be appointed by the Dictator from the elite in science, economics, finance and industry.

"We must infiltrate the youth of all classes to corrupt them and to teach them false principles.

"Existing laws need not be changed, but they can be rendered confusing and subject to arbitration.

"We will set up underground forces to prevent the *goyim* from rising up in arms against us."

Thus we see the existence of a well thought out plan for world domination. Rothschild then financed the Order of Illuminati, to be discussed in the next chapter. Near the end of the 19th century, Zionism arose. The *Protocols of the Learned Elders of Zion* appeared on the scene, containing many of Rothschild's ideas.

Meyer Amschel Rothschild established his first bank in Frankfurt in 1798, starting what was to become the greatest banking empire of all time. He trained his five sons in the banking business. Near the end of his life, he instructed his sons to establish banks in the major cities of Europe. Amschel, the eldest, was put in charge of the existing bank in Frankfurt, Germany. Salomon was sent to Vienna, Austria, Nathan to London, England, Charles to Naples, Italy and James to Paris, France.

Nathan turned out to be the most successful. He established N. M. Rothschild & Sons in London, a bank which exists to this day, as does the Paris bank. Nathan is famous for making a fortune on the bond market after the defeat of Napoleon at Waterloo, using his superior intelligence network to get news of the battle before it became commonly known.

The Rothschilds are famous for their passion of keeping their activities secret from the public. They do things through others. Their wealth is not disclosed in any magazines or financial newspapers. They have always worked together as a family and have not let outsiders become principals in their banks. They have always worked closely with other major international bankers, Jewish or otherwise.

They specialize in making large loans to governments. They create demand for loans by creating financial panics, depressions, famines, wars and revolutions.

They were instrumental in creating the Round Table groups in England through their agent, Lord Alfred Milner. These groups led to the creation of the Royal Institute of International Affairs in the United Kingdom, the Council on Foreign Relations in the United States and similar organizations throughout the English-speaking world. Today these groups are the primary vehicle which the Rothschilds use to communicate their orders to the national governments.

Thus we see the existence of a well thought out plan for world domination. Rothschild then financed the Order of Illuminati. Near the end of the 19th century, Zionism arose. The Protocols of the Learned Elders of Zion appeared on the scene, containing many of Rothschild's ideas.

An Illuminati religious ritual

CHAPTER 15

The Order of Illuminati

In order to further his plan for world domination, Meyer Amschel Rothschild financed a group called the Order of Illuminati, sometimes called the Bavarian Illuminati to distinguish it from other Illuminist groups.

Illuminati is a Latin word meaning enlightened or illuminated. In modern practice it has become a collective term for any group of elitists who pursue the New World Order and global governance by the rich and powerful.

The Order of Illuminati was formed by Adam Weishaupt on May 1, 1776. As a result, May 1 is an important date to this day in Illuminist and Communist circles.

Adam Weishaupt was originally a Jew, being born to Jewish parents. He was educated by Jesuits and converted to Catholicism, at least nominally. In reality, he was an atheist. He became Professor of Canon Law at the University of Ingolstadt in Bavaria, a Jesuit institution.

This was a group of free thinkers, modeled somewhat on the earlier Rosicrucians and the Spanish Aluminados. Weishaupt was a Freemason and used their idea of a series of degrees, in this case thirteen degrees leading to Rex (King) at the top of the pyramidal hierarchy. Its ideas go back to the mystery schools of ancient Greece and Egypt, as does Freemasonry. Each member was given a secret code name.

The organization had several basic goals:
- The destruction of Christianity and all monarchies.
- The destruction of nations in favor of internationalism.
- The discouragement of national patriotism in favor of universal brotherhood.
- The abolition of family ties and marriage.
- The suppression of private property rights and inheritance.

Weishaupt linked his group to Freemasonry at the Masonic convention at Wilhelmsbad in 1782, creating Illuminated Freemasons, a secret society within a secret society.

The organization was exposed by a freak accident in 1785. One of its members, Jacob Lang, was struck by lightning and killed. Secret papers about the Illuminati were found on his person. That led to searches of other members' homes. The Elector of Bavaria was shocked to learn of the subversive nature of the group and banned its further existence in 1786, just ten years after it was founded.

That was by no means the end of Illuminism, however. Organizations may go out of existence and individuals will die sooner or later, but ideas go on forever. The work of the Order was carried on in reading societies and subscription libraries. They influenced printing houses, bookseller shops and newspapers. One offshoot was the Jacobin Society, which was instrumental in setting off the French Revolution in 1789, one of Rothschild's objectives.

Two writers of the time wrote exposes of the Illuminati. In 1797 Abbe Augustin de Barruel traced Freemasonry and the Illuminati back to the Manicheans, who had been declared heretics in the 3rd century A.D. He also wrote about the Jacobins and their involvement in the French Revolution.

In 1798, John Robison, who was Professor of Natural Philosophy at the University of Edinburgh, wrote *Proofs of a Conspiracy Against All the Religions and Governments of Europe by Freemasons, Illuminati and Reading Societies.*

In later years, many organizations were formed to carry out the goal of world government by the elite. Among these are the Ordo Templi Orientis, Golden Dawn, Skull & Bones, Bohemian Society and many others. Nesta Webster identified many of them in her 1924 book, *Secret Societies and Subversive Movements.*

Today modern Illuminists are very active in preparing for the final steps toward world domination. They are preparing selected children for leadership positions. Those who will be the enforcers are being trained in crowd control and military tactics. They control all sources of information reaching the public. Mind control is being applied to the general public so that they will actually welcome the taking of power. Resisters will be imprisoned or killed. They planned and conducted the terrorist attacks of September 11, 2001 to advance their agenda. When the time is right, they will cause a financial collapse, which will cause many governments to collapse. Panic will set in. They will declare a state of emergency and declare martial law. A new monetary system will be introduced. Millions of "useless eaters" will be slaughtered. Their long-awaited millennium may be close at hand.

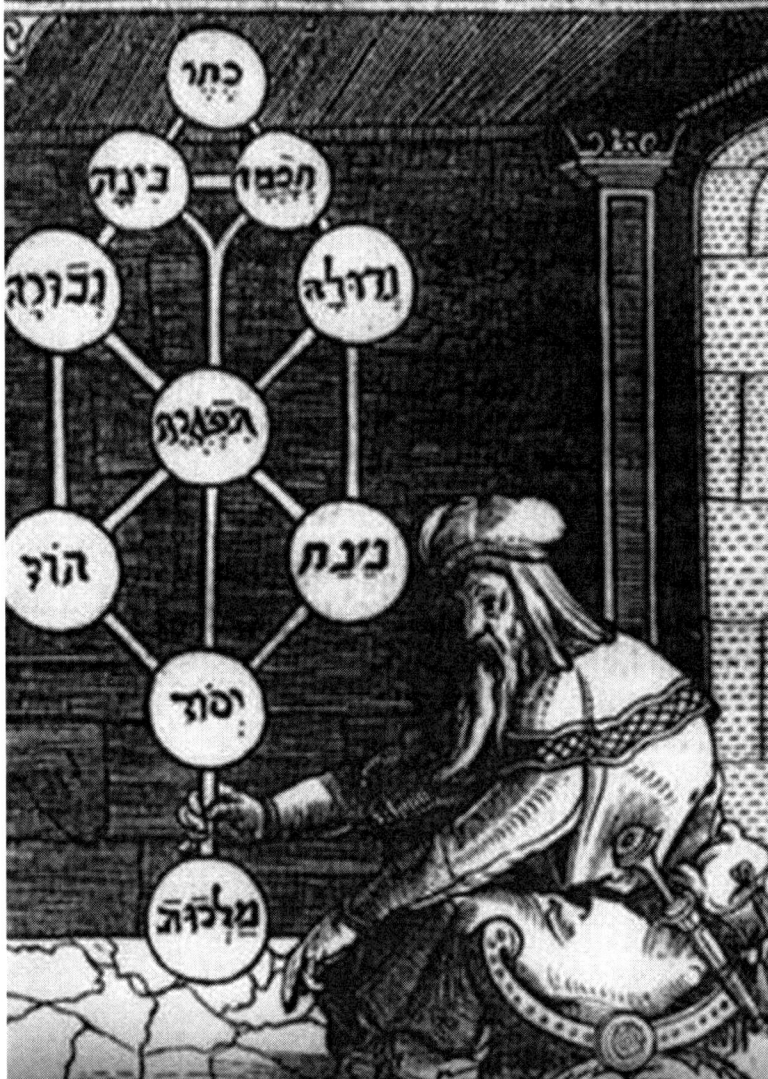

The Kabbalah "Tree of Life"

CHAPTER 16

Kabbalah

Kabbalah is the Hebrew word meaning tradition. It is sometimes thought to be an evil thing, linked to black magic and various heresies, but in reality it is an attempt to experience the living God by means of silent prayer, meditation, contemplation or other means. It is part of the broad field of mysticism, which is part of all the major religions, including Christianity, Islam, Hinduism, Confucianism, Buddhism and Taoism. Kabbalah is just the Jewish version of mysticism.

The Hebrew Bible is the principal source of Western mysticism's premises and symbolism. All the true Prophets had a mystical experience in which they experienced the divine, either by direct contact with God, an angel or in a heavenly vision. Those involved include Adam, Abraham, Jacob, Joseph, Moses, Isaiah, Ezekiel, Daniel, Hosea and Jeremiah.

Mysticism has a very long history, from before biblical times to the present. I include it in this part of the book because it was most prominent in the Middle Ages in all three monotheistic Western religions.

Kabbalah borrows ideas from many ancient sources in addition to the Hebrew Bible, including the ancient mystery schools, Gnosticism, Hermeticism, Zoroastrianism, astrology and magic. This is why people of orthodox beliefs tend to be suspicious of Kabbalah and of mysticism generally.

Kabbalah has influenced many other systems, including Neo-Platonism, Rosicrucianism, Freemasonry, Manichaeism, Albigensianism and Hasidism.

After the biblical times, Judaism entered what may be called the Hellenistic period, roughly 323 B.C. to A.D. 200. Apocalyptic literature was prominent during this period. The Essenes were a fundamentalist Jewish sect, with some of them living monastic lives. Hellenistic Jews, such as Philo of Alexandria, interpreted scripture allegorically.

The Prophet Ezekiel had a vision of *merkabah*, the heavenly throne chariot. This became part of the period in which the Talmud was written. The *Mishna* of Judah ha-Nasi, which codified the oral tradition of the Torah, was written about A.D. 200. Added to it was the *Gemara*, or commentary. The Palestinian version of the Talmud was completed in the 4th century and the longer and more influential Babylonian Talmud was completed in the fifth century. In the Orthodox Jewish community, the Talmud became more important than the Torah itself.

In the Middle Ages, the *Sefer Hasidim* (Book of the Devout), by Eleazar ben Jehudah of Worms (1160-1238) was very influential. It was written during the period of the Crusades, in which Jews were persecuted, especially in the Peasants Crusade. It reflects a deep personal piety and is less scholarly and speculative that earlier Kabbalah writings. It led to a form of mysticism known as the *Hasidei Ashkenazi* (the Pious of Germany).

Rabbi Moses ben Maimon, known as Maimonides or Rambam (1135-1204) was a Spanish Jewish philosopher and Talmudist. He was born in Cordova, fled to Morocco during a persecution of Jews by the Berbers and finally to Cairo, where he became physician to the sultan, Saladin. He sought to reconcile Jewish thought with the Aristotelian philosophy as presented by contemporary Arab writers. He wrote the *Mishneh Torah*, which codified rabbinic law and ritual. His best known work was The

Guide for the Perplexed, written to reconcile reason with faith. He commented on the 10th century *Book of Creation*, about the *sefirot*, the emanations from God. He influenced Albertus Magnus and Thomas Aquinas.

Prophetic Kabbalah was developed by Rabbi Abraham Abulafia (1240-1291). He met with Pope Nicholas III in 1280.

The most famous book of Kabbalist literature was the *Zohar* (Book of Splendor), by Moses de Leon (d. 1305), a Spanish Jewish mystic. He studied Maimonides, Torah, Talmud and earlier Kabbalah literature. This scholarly book was 2,400 pages in length, with 22 compositions. It describes the system of *sefirot*. It also describes *tikkun olam*, the healing of the world, a key part of the messianic system.

The Lurianic School of Kabbalah was based on the work of Isaac Luria (1534-1572). He wrote in reaction to the Inquisition. His *Book of Visions* emphasized personal asceticism and practical mysticism. He emphasized concentration or withdrawal, breaking the vessels and mending or uniting. He sought to bring about the messianic age. His beliefs included transmigration of souls, where after death, the soul would go to another person, rather than remain in paradise.

An interesting story of Jewish mysticism is the work of Rabbi Judah Loew (1525-1609), the Maharal of Prague and later chief rabbi of Poland. In 1586, we are told, he created a monster from the mud of the Moldau River to protect Jews from the Hapsburg emperor. He made it a living creature by placing the *shem* parchment, with God's name written on it, in its mouth. Eventually the monster turned on the Jews and its creator, who removed the *shem* from its mouth to kill it. The story later became the basis for Mary Shelly's novel, *Frankenstein's Monster*.

Messianic mysticism was largely the work of Sabbatai Zevi (1626-1676), a self-proclaimed Messiah and the founder of Sabbatianism. This is such an important subject that I will devote the next chapter to it.

A contrarian view was held by Benedict de Spinoza, also known as Baruch Spinoza (1632-1677), a Dutch Jew of Spanish descent. He read a lot and developed unorthodox pantheistic views, for which he was expelled from the synagogue. He was critical of Judaism and Christianity and a forerunner of biblical criticism.

New Hasidism was begun by Rabbi Israel ben Eliezer (1698-1760), who was called Ba'al Shem Tov (Master of the Good Name), or Besht for short. He developed a popular form of Kabbalah. He lived during the period of *Haskalah* or Enlightenment, when the beliefs of all traditional religions were threatened by scientific discoveries. We will look at this in Chapter 18. Hasidism was more popular in rural areas than in the larger cities.

Jacob Frank (1726-1791) was a follower of Sabbatai Zevi and another false messiah. We will discuss him in the next chapter.

Hasidic Kabbalah led eventually to Chabad Lubavitcher, a powerful ultra-conservative modern Orthodox movement. In the opposite direction, the Reform and Conservative movements of Judaism developed. The Reform movement rejected the Talmud and the all-powerful rabbinate and resorted to the Torah as the basis of religious beliefs. The Conservatives stand between the Orthodox and Reform positions.

Zionism, which we will discuss in a later chapter, is a secular form of messianism.

Kabbalah continues to exist in modern times. Recent writers include Martin Buber (1878-1965) and Abraham Joshua Heschel (1907-1972).

As was mentioned earlier, mysticism is found in all the major religions. In Christianity, there are literally dozens of examples of people who had contact with the divine, starting with Jesus, who was spoken to by God during his baptism and again at his transfiguration, according to Christian beliefs. Saul/Paul converted to Christianity after having a vision of Jesus. John of Patmos wrote the Book of Revelation based in part on his vision of heaven.

Other Christian mystics include John Cassian, Benedict of Nursia, Bernard of Clairvaux, Hildegard of Bingen, Francis of Assisi, Dominic of Calaruega, Albertus Magnus, Thomas Aquinas, Julian of Norwich, Thomas a Kempis, Ignatius of Loyola, Teresa of Avila, Philip Jakob Spener, Thomas Merton and Pierre Teilhard de Chardin, to name just a few.

Islam has its share of mystics also, starting with Muhammad, who learned the word of God from the angel Gabriel, according to Islamic beliefs. The Shi'a sect is largely mystic. Sufism is the Islamic form of mysticism. Famous Muslim mystics include Avicenna, Averoes, al Ghazzali, Ibn al-Arabi and al-Wahhab.

If you harbor negative thoughts about mysticism, hopefully this brief survey will put your mind at rest.

Sabbatai Levi

CHAPTER 17

The Sabbateans

The Sabbateans are a satanic Jewish cult who worship Lucifer, rather than Jahweh. They hate the true religious Jews and religious Jews hate the Sabbateans. They are a rich and powerful elite who are the prime movers in the New World Order and globalization.

To accomplish their agenda, they corrupt and undermine others' race, religion, nation and family. Their program includes sexual liberation, sexual promiscuity, interracial sex, independence for women, adultery, incest, internationalism and cultural diversity.

They encourage other Jews to convert to Christianity and to adopt Christian names in order to subvert Christianity from within. They encourage assimilation of other Jews into the nations where they live, rather than preserving their Jewish identity.

They were active in the Enlightenment, secularism and modernism. They started the Reform and Conservative schools of Judaism. They are the cult of the all-seeing eye of Horus, a symbol found on the seal of the United States and the $1 bill.

Two of their basic beliefs are "do as you will" and "the end justifies the means." They plan to exterminate many of the Gentiles when they complete the quest for global power and control.

Their movement was founded by Sabbatai Zevi (1626-1676), a deviant Kabbalist and self-proclaimed Messiah. He was born in Smyrna, Asia Minor (modern Turkey). He studied the Talmud, Kabbalah and Isaac Luria. He married and was divorced twice for his extreme asceticism. He had violent mood swings, from exaltation to melancholy, what we would call today a manic-depressive disorder.

In 1648, at age 22, he claimed to be the Messiah. He pronounced the divine name, JHWH, in public, a blasphemous act by Jewish standards. He was excommunicated by the rabbis. In 1651, he was banished from his native land. He wandered through the Mediterranean world, settling in Istanbul in 1653-1659.

He was very charismatic and had a sweet singing voice. He gave candy to children and prayed at the graves of saints. He thus attracted many disciples.

Eventually he was banished from Istanbul and went to Cairo, then Jerusalem and then back to Cairo. He married a woman named Sarah, who was a survivor of a pogrom in Europe and who made her living as a prostitute.

He met Nathan of Gaza, who became his advocate and promoter. Nathan announced in 1665 that the messianic age would begin in 1666 and that Sabbatai Zevi embodied Elijah and would conquer the world without bloodshed and would lead the ten lost tribes of Israel back to Israel. The rabbis in Jerusalem rejected this claim.

Zevi returned to Smyrna in 1665 and again proclaimed himself to be the Messiah. Some of his followers sold their houses in preparation to move to Jerusalem. He issued decrees to change the observance of Jewish laws, some of them quite extreme. For example, he decreed that Yom Kippur, the Day of Atonement and the most solemn day in the Jewish calendar, should be a day of rejoicing.

Zevi was arrested by the Muslim ruler of Istanbul for trying to overthrow the Sultan. He was tried in 1666 by Sultan Mehmed IV and imprisoned in Gallipoli. He was given the choice of dying as a Jewish martyr, or converting to Islam. He chose to convert. He became an Ismaili Shiite and a minor official. In succeeding years, he took on several more wives.

He lived another 10 years, during which time hundreds of thousands of Jews became his followers, expecting the immanent end times. A number of Muslims joined him also, forming a Judeo-Turkish sect called the Sabbateans.

He died in 1676. His followers expect him to return someday. Some believe that his soul transmigrated to Mayer Amschel Rothschild, a devout Jew. More likely, Rothschild knew of the Sabbateans from his Jewish connections and became a Sabbatean by that means.

In the 18th century, Sabbateanism was promoted by Jacob Frank (1726-1791), a contemporary of Mayer Amschel Rothschild. Sabbateans are sometimes called Frankists because of his efforts. Frank was excommunicated by the Jewish leaders in 1756.

The Sabbateans are part of the antinomianism movement, which also infects Christianity. The term was coined by Martin Luther and means against the law of God. In the case of the Judaism, it means rejection of God's law, as set forth in the Torah. In the case of Christianity, the idea goes back to Paul's teaching that salvation could be achieved by faith alone. Divine grace relieves the believer of the obligation to obey the moral law. Holy living is not necessary, according to this view. Of course, this idea could lead to anarchy and immorality. Unfortunately, it is a common view in the United States today.

I sincerely hope that this explanation will clarify some important issues relating to the relationship of Judaism to other faiths. While it is true that a tiny percentage of so-called Jews worship Lucifer rather than Jahweh and have decidedly evil beliefs, the vast majority of Jews cling to their Biblical heritage, as do Christians and Muslims. God forbid that there should be a holocaust in America where the many are penalized for the sins of the few.

OLIVER CROMWELL IN FRONT OF THE COFFIN OF CHARLES I

CHAPTER 18

The Enlightenment

The Enlightenment was a period in European history from about 1650 to 1800 where scientific reasoning had a profound effect on traditional religious and philosophical beliefs. It used the tools of science and mathematics, critical methods of modern biblical scholarship and the comparative study of religions. It emphasized reason over faith, rationality over tradition. Many freethinkers came to the fore, among them some of the most gifted thinkers of all time. Many Jewish and Christian teachings were challenged.

Deism was a widely held belief. It held that God had created the universe, then abandoned it to run in accordance with natural laws. This contrasted with the earlier belief that God remained in control of the world and continued to govern human behavior.

The Enlightenment followed the Thirty Years War (1618-1648), where Catholic nations such as Germany, Spain and Austria fought against Protestant nations such as England, France and Denmark, with neither side emerging as the clear winner. The Treaty of Westphalia was the settlement. During this time, the English Civil War was fought (1642-1652) and the monarchy under Charles I was temporarily deposed. Oliver Cromwell ruled England as the Lord Protector (1653-1658). After a brief rule by Cromwell's son Richard, Charles II gained the throne in 1660.

Toward the end of the Enlightenment, the American War of Independence from England was fought (1775-1783), as was the

French Revolution (1789-1799). The Order of Illuminati, discussed earlier, was formed in 1776.

Now let us consider some of the best-known thinkers of this period.

Rene Descartes (1596-1650) was a French philosopher. He had a Jesuit education, but he nevertheless believed that to discover the truth, it is necessary to abandon authority and tradition. We should take nothing for granted until it has been proved completely. He traveled extensively. He sought to reduce all of nature to mathematical laws, but he did not reject ethics and religion. He believed that God must exist and offered ontological (the branch of metaphysics dealing with the nature of being) arguments to support this position. He believed that mind and body are separate.

Blaise Pascal (1623-1662) was a French mathematician, physicist and philosopher. He was a mathematical genius from childhood. He was influenced by Jansenism, a movement which sought to reform the Roman Catholic Church and which held Augustine's views of predestination and grace. He believed that science is autonomous from philosophy. Man is meant for infinity. Reason and induction in the study of nature are completely subordinated to fact and must be proved by rigorous experimentation. He had a vision of God and surrendered to Jesus Christ. Yet he attacked the Jesuits for moral laxity. He stated "The Wager": Since faith is as reasonable as unbelief, why not bet our lives on the existence of God?

Baruch (Benedict de) Spinoza (1632-1677) was a Dutch Jewish philosopher whose ancestors had emigrated from Spain. He was brought up in the Orthodox Jewish community in Amsterdam, but held unorthodox views and was excommunicated in 1656. He synthesized Renaissance science with Greek, Stoic, Neo-Platonic and Scholastic philosophy. He thought of the cosmos as infinite. He accepted the heliocentric theory of the solar system. He believed God to be the dynamic principal of order, immanent within nature, rather than the transcendent creator of the universe. He originated the theory of parallelism of body and mind—the mind is subject to determinate laws of activity. Human salvation is based on a rational, universal system, not supernatural sanctions or revelations.

John Locke (1632-1704) was an English philosopher. He was a friend of Anthony Cooper, the Earl of Shaftesbury, a liberal spokesman and opponent of King Charles II and James II. Locke opposed the divine right of kings and supported the idea of a social contract, wherein the consent of the people is the basis of any sovereign's right to rule, which he held in trust and could be removed. He was a member of the Church of England, but a hedonist. He believed that the New Testament showed the way to long-term happiness. He supported the Glorious Revolution which brought William of Orange to the English throne. He believed that religious ideas should be clear, simple and within the bounds of reason.

Philipp Jacob Spener (1635-1705) was a German theologian and founder of the Pietist Movement. He disliked a lifeless orthodoxy. He believed that justification came by faith alone. Pietism was a reform movement within Lutheranism, based on true faith, repentance, conversion and rebirth, rather than scholastic theology. He was supported by Count Nicholas Ludwig von Zinzendorf (1700-1760), founder of the Moravian Church.

Sir Isaac Newton (1642-1727) was an English physicist, mathematician and natural philosopher. He invented the differential calculus. He formulated the laws of universal gravitation, orbits of the planets and optics and invented the reflecting telescope. He was a Fellow, and later president, of the Royal Society and grand master of the Priory of Zion, 1691-1727. He believed that God was the author and creator of all things.

William Penn (1644-1718) was an English Quaker. He engaged in oral and written religious and political agitation. He founded the city of Philadelphia as the city of brotherly love. He founded the State of Pennsylvania, which he called a holy experiment.

Francois-Marie Arouet de Voltaire (1694-1788) was a French philosopher, historian, novelist, dramatist and poet. He joined the Society of the Temple, a free-thinking and dissolute society around the Duke of Vendome, Grand Prior of the Knights of Malta. A Deist, he moved to England in 1726, where he satirized Quakers, Anglicans and Presbyterians alike. His whole life was devoted to protesting existing evils. He believed there was no such thing as divine benevolence; bad things happen to everybody, especially natural disasters.

John Wesley (1703-1791) was an English clergyman, a priest in the Church of England. With his brother, Charles Wesley (1707-1788), he founded the Holy Club at Oxford to promote frequent attendance at the sacraments. Although John was raised as a High Church Anglican, he preferred simpler liturgy and a religion of the heart. Charles wrote many church hymns. Both remained Anglican priests all their lives, but they are considered to be the founders of Methodism.

David Hume (1711-1776) was a Scottish Presbyterian philosopher, historian and writer. He studied human nature and developed a rigorous philosophy of skepticism in an age of reason. He felt belief is not susceptible to demonstration. He distinguished between the realm of the absolute and the realm of experience and knowledge versus belief. He felt that religion originates in man's hopes and fears, not in philosophy.

Jean-Jacques Rousseau (1712-1778) was a French philosopher. His deistic ideas irritated the Roman Catholic Church. He revolted against conventionality, superficiality, greed and the accumulation of wealth. He believed that there is no such thing as original sin and thus there is no need for a savior. Man is good by nature, corrupted by society and constantly in search of a higher self through a rational religion.

Immanuel Kant (1724-1804) was a German philosopher, born to Lutheran Pietist parents. He wrote *Critique of Pure Reason* in 1781. He believed that a valid religious belief can derive only from the implications of moral principles and the nature of moral life, but on these grounds it is rationally required. He criticized clericalism and state religions.

Moses Mendelssohn (1729-1786) was a Jewish German philosopher and a friend of Immanuel Kant. He translated the Torah into German. He was the grandfather of the famous composer, Felix Mendelssohn-Bartholdy.

Johann Wolfgang von Goethe (1749-1832) was a German poet, dramatist and novelist. He is best known for his drama *Faust*, which portrays a man tempted by the Devil. Faust makes a deal with the Devil, promising his soul in exchange for worldly successes. At Faust's death, saints and angels pray for his soul through the mercy of the benign Lord. Goethe placed less emphasis on the Bible and theology and more on nature, human sentiment and folk traditions.

Jewish cobblers in the Pale of Settlement

CHAPTER 19

The Pale of Settlement

The Pale of Settlement was set up by Russia in 1795 to serve as the place where Jews could live. It covered a large area, from the Black Sea to the Baltic Sea, including most of what today is Poland, Ukraine and Belarus. A brief review of Polish history would be pertinent.

In 1226, the Teutonic Knights conquered most of what later became East Prussia and later still, part of Germany. In 1241, the Mongol invasions of Europe began.

In Poland in 1251, the Statute of Kalisz gave Jews many rights, including their own legal system, the Kahal. In 1347, the Statutes of Wislica allowed more Jews to settle in Poland. In the 15th century, many cities, or even entire countries, expelled Jews from their territory. Many of them emigrated to Poland. They did not try to assimilate, but formed a state within a state.

Due to their characteristic excellence, some Jews became advisers to the Polish nobility. Others became tax farmers, which made them unpopular with the people. King Sigismund II August (ruled 1548-1572) surrounded himself with Jews and also with Protestant revolutionaries. King Bathory (ruled 1575-1586) further expanded the privileges of the Jews.

The region was grain-producing. Jews managed to build a monopoly in vodka production, as well as usury. This allowed them to control grain prices and to exploit the alcoholism of the farmers. This added to resentment against the Jews.

In 1648, Bogdan Chmielnicki, the leader of the Cossacks, led a revolt against the Jews in Poland, which soon spread to the surrounding areas. He defeated the Polish army at first and the revolt was not put down until 1656. In the meantime, more than 100,000 Jews were killed in this pogrom. Many Jews left Poland and moved west, especially to Hamburg and Amsterdam.

Over the next century, Poland grew in size, expanding into what is today parts of Ukraine, Belarus and the Crimea. Many Jews emigrated to Poland. By 1772, more than 80% of the Jews in the world lived there.

In 1772, Poland was partitioned, with parts of it going to Russia, Prussia and Austria. The westernmost section of Russia became known as the Pale of Settlement. A second partitioning in 1793 took away more territory. In 1795, as a result of a third partitioning, Poland ceased to exist as a nation. It did not again become a sovereign nation until after World War I.

As a result of the partitioning, Russia now had about 50% of the world's Jewish population within its borders. Most of these were descendants of the Khazars, rather than the Israelites.

Russia had a long history of "Jewish problems." In 1795, the Pale of Settlement law was enacted in Russia. Jews were legally required to live in that area and thus Jews living in the rest of Russia were forced to move into it. As noted above, this was a very large area, extending from the Black Sea to the Baltic Sea.

In 1815, after the Napoleonic Wars, central Poland became part of the Russian Empire, adding another 400,000 Jews to Russia's population.

By 1880, over 4,000,000 Jews lived in the Pale. Many of them were driven out by a long series of pogroms. Over the next 30 years, about 2,000,000 of them emigrated to the United States, especially New York City, where they became an important economic and political force.

The Pale of Settlement was set up by Russia in 1795 to serve as the place where Jews could live. It covered a large area, from the Black Sea to the Baltic Sea, including most of what today is Poland, Ukraine and Belarus.

Karl Marx

CHAPTER 20

Communism

Communism as we know it today is based largely on the *Communist Manifesto*, which was drafted by Moses Hess and published by Karl Marx and Friedrich Engels in 1848. Some of its underlying ideas go back many centuries.

The Greek philosophers Pythagoras and Plato had ideas on the subject. Plato believed that the worst social evils—war and poverty—were caused by the accumulation of wealth by the ruling class, hence wealth should be more evenly distributed. The Franciscan friars pooled their property. The English Peasants Revolt of 1381 claimed that land should be held in common for the peasants and not owned by kings, nobles, or landlords.

Sir Thomas More wrote *Utopia* in 1516, advocating common ownership of property. The German Peasants War of 1524-1525, led by Thomas Munzer, held that there should be no private property.

The French Revolution of 1789, led by Robespierre and the Jacobins, advocated the centralization of political power in the control of the masses. Robert Owen predicted that workers would create the institutions for a future communistic society. Louis Blanc expressed the idea that income should be taken from each according to his capacities and given to each according to his needs. Louis Feuerbach advocated an atheistic materialism.

Jews were the inventors of modern communism and are its

leaders to this day. Karl Marx (1818-1883), a German economist, came from a long line of Jewish rabbis, although he himself was an atheist. He dismissed God as irrelevant, not able to help humanity. He described religion as a fiction which makes life bearable for the oppressed—the opiate of the masses. Judaism was no longer a religion, he said, but a worldly cult of the Jews, whose God was money. Of course the same thing could be said of a number of Christians today.

Friedrich Engels (1826-1895) also was a German economist. He studied the works of Moses Hess and converted to communism. He became a long-time collaborator of Karl Marx.

In 1847, the Communist League commissioned the writing of a manifesto of their principles. Moses Hess wrote the first draft. Marx and Engels completed it and published it in February 1848. They wrote of alienation, in which labor sells itself to capitalists, who then own the product and the profits from it.

That situation, they said, would lead to class struggle, then to a dictatorship of the proletariat and finally to a classless society. Production would progress from slavery to feudalism to capitalism to communism.

The Jewish elite saw communism as a way to gain control of the world from the bottom up—revolution of the working class proletariat against the bourgeoisie middle class and the ruling class. It was another means of achieving Jewish supremacy over the hated Gentiles. Later in the 19th century, Jews developed Zionism, a plan to gain world control from the top down. We will discuss that movement in the next chapter.

There are ten planks to the *Communist Manifesto*. It is interesting to see how many of them have been introduced into the United States over the years, always in the name of liberalism.

The first plank called for the abolition of property rights in land and the application of all rents of land to public purposes. We still allow private ownership of land, but we require the payment of property taxes on it, with confiscation if the taxes are not paid. Also, much of the land in the United States is owned by the government. In many western states, the majority of the land is publicly owned.

The second plank called for a progressive income tax. We have had this since 1913, even though it is unconstitutional.

The third plank called for the abolition of all right of inheritance. While we still allow inheritance, it is subject to inheritance tax, estate tax and gift tax.

The fourth plank called for confiscation of the property of all emigrants and rebels. We have tax levies, property seizures and fines by the Internal Revenue Service. The government seizes any property suspected to be involved in drug trading. We have had numerous raids on private property, including Waco, Ruby Ridge and the Montana Freemen.

Fifth, Marx and Engels called for the consolidation of credit in the hands of the state, by means of a national bank with state capital. We have gone beyond this by creation of the Federal Reserve System, a privately owned bank which is authorized to create money out of thin air and charge us interest on it. We will discuss this in a later chapter.

The sixth plank called for the centralization of the means of communication and transport in the hands of the state. We require our citizens to have drivers licenses and vehicle registrations. There are numerous federal agencies regulating nearly all aspects of our lives, including the Federal Aviation Administration, Federal Communications Commission and the Interstate Commerce Commission.

Item seven called for the extension of factories and instruments of production owned by the state, the bringing into cultivation the waste lands and the improvement of the soil generally in accordance with a common plan. We have thousands of government regulations and requirements for licenses. In recent years the government has taken control of many businesses. We have the Department of Agriculture, the Tennessee Valley Authority and other large government projects.

The eighth plank called for equal liability of all to labor and the establishment of "industrial armies," especially for agriculture. We have several volunteer programs and have had the Civilian Conservation Corps, Works Progress Administration and the military draft.

The ninth item called for combination of agriculture with manufacturing industries and gradual abolition of the distinction between town and country by a more equitable distribution of population over the country. In America, small individually owned farms have all but disappeared and have been replaced by multinational agricultural conglomerates such as Archer Daniels Midland. Much of the population has moved from rural areas to cities and suburbs.

The tenth plank called for free education for all children in public schools, abolition of children's factory labor and combination of education with industrial production. We have public schools, vocational schools and child labor laws.

A certain element within Judaism has been interested in leading revolutions. Karl Marx was one of these. He was one of the leaders of the Revolution of 1848 in Germany, which also occurred in Belgium, Austria, Hungary, Italy, France and Denmark, all led by Jews and coordinated by the Talmudic rabbinate.

The First International, also called the International Working Men's Association, lasted from 1864 to 1872. In 1871, the Paris Commune led an unsuccessful revolt.

When communists found that their movement was resisted, they called it socialism instead, or more recently liberalism. It's amazing how easy it is to deceive the *goyim* by changing the name of things. In 1875, the Social Democratic Party formed in Germany under the control of communists.

The Second International lasted from 1889 to 1914. Its objective was to bring more and more of the economy under the control or ownership of the national state. The Third International was formed in 1919.

In 1917, the Russian Revolution occurred, also called the October Revolution or Bolshevik Revolution. It was almost entirely a Jewish-led affair. Civil war lasted from 1918 to 1921, with the Reds versus the Whites. An elite called the *nomenklatura* took power. We will discuss this further in a later chapter.

Lenin died in 1924. Stalin gradually took power. Trotsky was exiled and later killed.

During World War II, the Soviet Union joined the Allied Nations against Germany, Italy and Japan and won most of Eastern Europe for its efforts.

After World War II, international alliances shifted radically. The Cold War began, with the excuse for war being described as capitalism versus communism. The Cold War lasted until 1990, when the Soviet Union broke up. We were told that communism was dead. Nothing could be further than the truth. In the former Soviet Union, many of the same people are still in charge, albeit under new party names. China, Viet Nam, Cambodia and North Korea are clearly communist nations, as are the Central Asian "stans"—Kazakhstan, Uzbekistan, Turkmenistan, Kyrgystan and Tajikstan.

In Latin America, Cuba is clearly communistic and several other nations—Venezuela, Brazil, Colombia, Bolivia, Ecuador, Nicaragua, Uruguay, Paraguay, El Salvador and Mexico—have come under communistic influence.

Let us next turn our attention to another primarily Jewish development: Zionism.

Theodor Herzl

CHAPTER 21

Zionism

Moses Hess (1812-1875), one of the founders of communism, was also a leader in the Zionist movement. In 1862, he advocated the establishment of a Zionist government in Palestine.

The initial objective of Zionism was to establish a Jewish homeland in Palestine and to encourage as many Jews as possible in the diaspora to settle there. Once a foothold was established, the territory could gradually be extended to become Greater Israel, the land from the Nile to the Euphrates, which God had promised to the Israelites in biblical times. Eventually the Messianic age would be established, with Israel ruling the world from Jerusalem.

The concept of world domination by Jews goes back to God's covenant with Abraham, reaffirmed to Isaac, Jacob, Moses and David. It was carried on from the Levite priests to the Pharisees to the rabbis to the Talmudists to the Zionists.

This idea was especially attractive to the Jews in Russia, who had been the victims of oppression for many years. Jews living in the United States, where they were prosperous and well-respected citizens, had little interest in emigrating to Palestine. Some Orthodox Jews felt that it was improper to try to regain control of Palestine until the Messiah came to lead the way.

Another problem was that the descendants of the Israelites, who had lived in Canaan (later called Palestine) in biblical times, constituted only about twenty percent of the world-wide Jewish population in the 19th century. The vast majority of Jews, descendants of the Khazars, never lived there, but came from a large area around the Caspian Sea. This problem was resolved by de-emphasizing the existence of the Khazars and by promoting a united front of all Jews.

Zionism was promoted by infiltrating the highest levels of society in order to gain control from the top down. It was the upper arm of the pincer, of which communism, moving from the bottom up, was the lower arm.

Zionism pursued a race-based colonialism, while communism envisioned an egalitarian utopia. Zionist leaders worked with the Fabian Socialists in the United Kingdom.

In 1896, Dr. Theodor Herzl, an Austrian author and journalist, wrote *The Jewish State*, which advocated a Jewish homeland in Palestine.

The First Zionist Conference met in Basel, Switzerland, in March 1897. The delegates drew up a set of 24 protocols to carry out their objectives, to be discussed in the next chapter. They created the World Zionist Organization. Dr. Herzl presided, but he was soon replaced by Dr. Chaim Weizmann, who was to lead the group for many years.

The British government offered Uganda, then a British colony, to the Zionists as a future homeland, but that offer was later rejected. The Zionists were intent on gaining Palestine.

Then as now, most of the Zionist leaders were wealthy Jews who had business and social contacts with Christian political leaders. In the United Kingdom, early supporters of Zionism included Alfred Balfour, Lloyd George and Winston Churchill.

In the United States, Rabbi Stephen Wise was the chief Zionist organizer. Other leading Zionists included Bernard Baruch, Louis Brandeis and Benjamin Cardoza. They gained the support of President Woodrow Wilson and his chief adviser, Edward Mandel House.

On November 2, 1917, Alfred Balfour, then Foreign Secretary

of the U. K., issued the Balfour Declaration to Lord Rothschild. It promised British support for a Jewish homeland in Palestine. At the time, Palestine was still part of the Ottoman Empire against which General Allenby was engaged in war. Palestine did not become a British mandate until 1922. Interestingly, Jews achieved another major goal that same week—the Bolshevik overthrow of the Czar in Russia.

In 1920, there were more than 800,000 Arab Muslims and Christians living in Palestine. Jews started emigrating there in small numbers, but were disliked by the native Palestinians. Battles broke out from time to time.

Many Jews left the Pale of Settlement, due to persecution by the Russians. Some went to Palestine, but the largest number by far went to the United States. In 1877, America was home to 230,000 Jews. By 1926, the number had increased to 4,500,000. Few American Jews were willing to give up a good life in America for the rigors and dangers in Palestine.

Hitler came to power in Germany in 1933. His anti-Semitic harangues struck fear in the hearts of German Jews. The World Jewish Congress declared economic war on Germany. Hitler responded by repressive measures against Jews. He proposed to offer the Jews a homeland in Madagascar, but that never came to pass. He made a deal with Lord Rothschild to transfer German Jews to Palestine, but not many went. He then began forcibly transporting them out of the country in massive numbers, mostly to Poland, where they became slave laborers and their property confiscated.

During World War II, Zionists in Palestine were secretly armed as part of the war effort. Increasing hostility of the Palestinians led to the formation of terrorists groups by the Jews, such as Irgun and the Stern Gang.

In 1948, the State of Israel was declared, fulfilling the primary Zionist goal. We will look at this in a later chapter.

CHAPTER 22

The Protocols

T he *Protocols of the Learned Elders of Zion* are one of the most important and most debated writings of all time. Their very origin as a Jewish document was denied at first, but later admitted.

No one individual claimed authorship. Apparently the version introduced at the First Zionist Conference in 1897 was the work of the Masonic Lodge of Mizraim in Paris. Adolph Cremieux, head of the lodge and Joseph Levy, a member, may have headed the effort. Other contributors may have included Lionel Rothschild, Moses Hess and Theodor Herzl.

The text itself tells of ancient origins of the ideas contained in the document and the work of many generations. Certain passages suggest that this version was written in France late in the 19th century.

The main theme is the methods by which the Jewish elite will gain control of the world by deceiving the Gentiles, who are referred to as the *goyim* in the original Hebrew version. The idea of world domination by the Jews as God's chosen people, as promised by God himself, goes back to the final version of the Torah, put together by a team led by the priest Ezra in 458 B.C.

The Babylonian Talmud, as expanded by the rabbis over the centuries, is another major source. Many of the ideas set forth by Mayer Amschel Rothschild in 1773 appear almost verbatim in the *Protocols*. The plans of the Bavarian Illuminati, led by Adam

Weishaupt, are also included.

The *Protocols* describe a work in progress, rather than a hopeful dream for the future. The writing is very professional and well thought out. It is not propaganda, nor is it an attempt to stir up antagonism.

The enemy is the Gentiles, not the aristocracy, government, or capitalists as such. The objective is control of the Gentiles of the world by the Jewish elite.

In 1905, a translation into Russian by Professor Sergei Nilus, a Russian Orthodox priest, was published. In the same year, an attempted revolution, led by Jews, was put down and many of the leaders were exiled, mostly going to the United States. The *Protocols* were denounced as a hoax and a fraud, intended to stir up hate against the Jews.

When the Jews came to power in Russia in 1917, one of the first acts was to make anti-Semitism a criminal offense. The *Protocols* were banned; anyone caught with a copy was severely punished. The ban later spread to the Soviet-controlled countries.

In 1920, Victor Marsden produced the first English translation. A series about the international Jew and discussing the *Protocols* appeared in the *Dearborn Independent*, a newspaper controlled by Henry Ford, who later wrote a book on the same subjects.

In 1923, Alfred Rosenberg, an associate of Adolph Hitler, wrote a German translation of the *Protocols*. Hitler referred to it in his book *Mein Kampf*, written in 1924-1925 when he was in prison. Hitler used the document in his criticism of the Jews.

The most convincing proof of the authenticity of the *Protocols* is that they describe what actually happened in the past and what is actually happening in the world today.

Let's now take a look at some of major provisions in the *Protocols*. I will quote portions of the English translation verbatim.

Protocol #1. It must be noted that men with bad instincts are more in number than the good and therefore the best results in governing them are attained by violence and terrorization and not by academic discussions. . . . I draw the conclusion that by the law of nature, right lies in force. Political freedom is an idea but not a fact. . . . In our day the power of the rulers who were liberal is the power of gold. Time was when faith ruled. . . . The despotism of capital, which is entirely in our hands, reaches out to it a straw that the state, willy-nilly, must take hold of; if not, it goes to the bottom. . . . The political has nothing in common with the moral. The ruler who is governed by the moral is not a skilled politician and is therefore unstable on his throne. . . . Our right lies in force. . . . The result justifies the means. . . . Only one trained from childhood for independent rule can have understanding of the words that can be made up of the political alphabet. . . . The peoples of the *goyim* are bemused with alcoholic liquors. . . . We must not stop at bribery, deceit and treachery when they should serve towards the attainment of our end. . . . It is not by the means themselves as by the doctrine of severity that we shall triumph and bring all governments into subjection to our super-government. . . . Far back in ancient times we were the first to cry among the masses of the people the words "Liberty, Equality and Fraternity." . . . And all the time these words were canker-worms boring into the well-being of the *goyim*, putting an end everywhere to peace, quiet, solidarity and destroying all the foundations of the *goyim* states.

Protocol #2. It is indispensable for our purpose that wars, so far as possible, should not result in territorial gains. War will thus be brought on to the economic ground, where the nations will not fail to perceive in the assistance we give the strength of our predominance. . . . Think carefully of the successes we arranged for Darwinism, Marxism, Nietzsche-ism. To us Jews, at any rate, it should be plain to see what a disintegrating importance these directives have had on the minds of the *goyim*. . . . Through the press we have gained the power to influence while remaining ourselves in the shade; thanks to the press we have got the gold in our hands.

Protocol #3. There remains a small space to cross and the whole long path we have trodden is now ready to close its cycle of the Symbolic Snake, by which we symbolize our people. When this ring closes, all the states of Europe will be locked in its coil as in a powerful vice. . . . All people are chained down to heavy toil by poverty more firmly than ever they were by slavery and serfdom. . . . The people have fallen into the grips of merciless money-grinding scoundrels who have laid a pitiless and cruel yoke upon the necks of the workers. . . . We appear on the scene as alleged saviors of the worker from this oppression. . . . We are interested in just the opposite—the killing off of the *goyim*. Our power is in the chronic shortage of food and physical weakness of the worker because by all that this implies he is made the slave of our will. When the hour strikes for our Sovereign Lord of all the world to be crowned, it is these same hands which will sweep away everything that might be a hindrance thereto. . . . We shall create by all the secret subterranean methods open to us and with the aid of gold, which is all in our hands, a universal economic crisis whereby we shall throw upon the streets whole mobs of workers simultaneously in all the countries of Europe. . . . Remember the French Revolution, to which it was we who gave the name of "Great": the secrets of its preparations are well known to us for it was wholly the work of our hands. Ever since that time we have been leading the peoples from one disenchantment to another, so that in the end they should turn also from us in favor of the King-Despot of the blood of Zion, whom we are preparing for the world.

Protocol #4. Who and what is in a position to overthrow an invisible force? And this is precisely what our force is. Gentile Freemasonry blindly serves as a screen for us and our objects, but the plan of action of our force, even its very abiding-place, remains for the whole people an unknown mystery. . . . It is indispensable for us to undermine all faith, to tear out of the mind of the *goyim* the very principle of God-head and the spirit and to put in its place arithmetical calculations and material needs.

Protocol #5. We shall create an intensified centralization of government in order to grip in our hands all the forces of the community. . . . Our kingdom will be distinguished by a despotism of such magnificent proportions as to be at any moment and in every place in a position to wipe out any *goyim* who oppose us by deed or word. . . . The nations cannot come to even an inconsiderable private agreement without our secretly having a hand in it. . . . And it was said by the prophets that we were chosen by God himself to rule over the whole Earth. God has endowed us with genius that we may be equal to our task. . . . All the wheels of the machinery of all states go by the force of the engine, which is in our hands and that engine of the machinery of states is—gold. . . . We must so direct the education of the *goyim* communities that whenever they come upon a matter requiring initiative they may drop their hands in despairing impotence.

Protocol #6. We shall soon begin to establish huge monopolies, reservoirs of colossal riches, upon which even large fortunes of the *goyim* will depend to such an extent that they will go to the bottom together with the credit of the states on the day after the political smash. . . . In every possible way we must develop the significance of our super-government by representing it as the protector and benefactor of all those who voluntarily submit to us. . . . What we want is that industry should drain off from the land both labor and capital and by means of speculation transfer into our hands all the money of the world and thereby throw all the *goyim* into the ranks of the proletariat.

Protocol #7. The intensification of armaments, the increase in police forces, are all essential for the completion of the aforementioned plans. What we have to get at is that there should be in all the states of the world, besides ourselves, only the masses of the proletariat, a few millionaires devoted to our interests, police and soldiers. . . . We must create ferments, discords and hostility. . . . The principal factor of success in the political is the secrecy of its undertakings. . . . We must compel the governments of the *goyim* to take action in the direction favored by our widely conceived plan...by what we shall represent as public opinion, secretly promoted by us through the means of that so-called "great power"—the press, which, with a few exceptions that may be disregarded, is already entirely in our hands.

Protocol #8. We must arm ourselves with all the weapons which our opponents might employ against us. . . . Our directorate...will surround itself with publicists, practical jurists, administrators, diplomats and finally, with persons prepared by special super-educational training in our special schools. . . . We shall surround our government with a whole world of economists. . . . Around us again will be a whole constellation of bankers, industrialists, capitalists, and—the main thing—millionaires, because in substance everything will be settled by the question of figures.

Protocol #9. The words of the liberal, which are in effect the words of our Masonic watchword, namely "Liberty, Equality and Fraternity," will, when we come into our kingdom, be changed by us into words no longer a watchword, but only an expression of idealism, namely into "The right of liberty, the duty of equality and the ideal of brotherhood.". . . If any states raise a protest against us, it is only *pro forma* at our discretion and by our direction, for their anti-Semitism is indispensable to us for the management of our lesser brethren. . . . And the weapons in our hands are limitless ambitions, burning greediness, merciless vengeance, hatreds and malice. . . . It is from us that the all-engulfing terror proceeds. . . . Division into fractional parties has given them into our hands, for, in order to carry on a contested struggle one must have money and the money is all in our hands. . . . We have got our hands into the administration of the law, into the conduct of elections, into the press, into liberty of the person, but principally into education and training as being the cornerstone of a free existence.

Protocol #10. I beg you to bear in mind that governments and people are content in the political with outside appearances. . . . We shall destroy among the *goyim* the importance of the family and its educational value and remove the possibility of individual minds splitting off. . . . A scheme of government should come ready made from one brain. . . . We want our schemes to be forcible and suitably concocted. Therefore we ought not to fling the work of genius of our guide to the fangs of the mob or even of a select company. . . . When we introduced into the State organism the poison of liberalism its whole political complexion underwent a change. . . . We shall arrange elections in favor of such presidents as have in their past some dark, undiscovered stain; then they will be trustworthy agents for the accomplishment of our plans out of fear of revelations and from the natural desire of everyone who has attained power, namely, the retention of the privileges, advantages and honor connected with the office of president. . . . Independently of this we shall invest the president with the right of declaring a state of war.

Protocol #11. This, then, is the program of the new constitution. We shall make law, right and justice (1) in the guise of proposals to the legislative corps, (2) by decrees of the president under the guise of general regulations, of orders of the Senate and of resolutions of the State Council in the guise of ministerial orders, (3) and in case a suitable occasion should arise—in the form of a revolution in the state. . . . The *goyim* are a flock of sheep and we are their wolves. . . . It is this which has served as the basis for our organization of secret Masonry which is not known to and aims which are not even so much as suspected by, these *goy* cattle, attracted by us into the "show" army of Masonic lodges in order to throw dust in the eyes of their fellows. . . . God has granted us, his Chosen People, the gift of the dispersion…which has now brought us to the threshold of sovereignty over all the world.

Protocol #12. We shall deal with the press in the following way…We shall saddle it and bridle it with a tight curb; we shall do the same also with all productions of the printing press. . . . We shall lay on it a special stamp tax and require deposits of caution-money before permitting the establishment of any organ of the press or of printing offices. . . . Not a single announcement will reach the public without our control. . . . Every one desirous of being a publisher, librarian, or printer, will be obliged to provide himself with the diploma instituted therefore, which, in case of any fault, will be immediately impounded. . . . Before accepting any production for publication in print, the publisher or printer will have to apply to the authorities for permission to do so. . . . Our government will become the proprietor of the majority of the journals.

Protocol #13. The need for daily bread forces the *goyim* to keep silence and be our humble servants. . . . Questions of the political are unattainable for any save those who have guided it already for many ages, the creators. . . . In order that the masses themselves may not guess what they are about, we further distract them with amusements, games, pastimes, passions, people's palaces. Soon we shall begin through the press to propose competitions in art, in sport of all kinds. . . . Who will ever suspect then that all these peoples were stage-managed by us according to a political plan which no one has so much as guessed at in the course of many centuries?

Protocol #14. When we come into our kingdom it will be undesirable for us that there should exist any other religion than ours of the One God with whom our destiny is bound up by our position as the Chosen People.... We must therefore sweep away all other forms of belief.... Our philosophers will discuss all the shortcomings of the various beliefs of the *goyim*, but none will ever bring under discussion our faith from its true point of view since this will be fully learned by none save ours who will never dare to betray its secrets.

Protocol #15. When we at last definitely come into our kingdom by the aid of *coups d'etat* prepared everywhere for one and the same day, after the worthlessness of all existing forms of government has been definitely acknowledged…we shall make it our task to see that against us such things as plots shall no longer exist. With this purpose we shall slay without mercy all who take arms (in hand) to oppose our coming into our kingdom. Every kind of new institution of anything like a secret society will also be punished with death. Those of them which are now in existence, are known to us, serve us and have served us, we shall disband and send into exile to continents far removed from Europe; in this way we shall proceed with those *goy* Masons who know too much.... Such was, until recent times, the Russian autocracy, the one and only serious foe we had in the world, without counting the Papacy.... Meantime... we shall create and multiply free Masonic lodges in all the countries of the world, absorb into them all who may become or who are prominent in public activity, for in these lodges we shall find our principal intelligence office and means of influence.... Among the members of these lodges will be almost all the agents of international and national police.... We shall root out liberalism from all the important strategic posts of our government on which depends the training of subordinates for our State structure.... All the money in the world will be concentrated in our hands; consequently it is not our government that has to fear expense.... Our government will have the appearance of a patriarchal paternal guardianship on the part of our ruler. Our own nation and our subjects will discern in his person a father caring for their every need, their every act, their every interrelation as subjects one with another, as well as their relations to the ruler.... We are obliged without hesitation to sacrifice individuals who commit a breach of established order, for in the exemplary punishment of evil lies a great educational problem.... When the King of Israel sets upon his sacred head the crown offered him by Europe, he will become patriarch of the world.

Protocol #16. In order to effect the destruction of all collective forces except ours, we shall emasculate the first state of collectivism—the universities—by re-educating them in a new direction. Their officials and professors will be prepared for their business by detailed secret programs of action from which they will not with impunity diverge, not by one iota. They will be appointed with especial precaution and will be so placed as to be wholly dependent on the government.... We will erase from the memory of men all facts of previous centuries which are undesirable to us.... We shall abolish every kind of freedom of instruction.... The system of bridling thought is already at work in the so-called system of teaching by object lessons, the purpose of which is to turn the *goyim* into unthinking submissive brutes.

Protocol #17. The practice of advocacy produces men cold, cruel, persistent, unprincipled, who in all cases take up a impersonal, purely legal standpoint...We shall set this profession into narrow frames which will keep it inside the sphere of executive public service. Advocates, equally with judges, will be deprived of the right of communication with litigants.... We have long past taken care to discredit the priesthood of the *goyim*.... Freedom of conscience has been declared everywhere, so that now only years divide us from the moment of the complete wrecking of that Christian religion.... The King of the Jews will be the real Pope of the Universe, the patriarch of the international Church.

... In our program, one-third of our subjects will keep the rest under observation from a sense of duty, on the principle of volunteer service to the state. It will then be no disgrace to be a spy and informer, but a merit.

Protocol #18. We have compelled the rulers to acknowledge their weakness in advertising overt measures of secret defense and thereby we shall bring the promise of authority to destruction. ... Criminals with us will be arrested at the first more or less well-grounded suspicion.

Protocol #19. If we do not permit any independent dabbling in the political we shall on the other hand encourage every kind of report or petition with proposals for the government to examine into all kinds of projects for the amelioration of the condition of the people. ... In order to destroy the prestige of heroism for political crime we shall send it for trial in the category of thieving, murder and every kind of abominable and filthy crime. ... We have advertised the martyrdom alleged to have been accepted by sedition-mongers for the idea of the commonweal. This advertisement has increased the contingent of liberals and has brought thousands of *goyim* into the ranks of our livestock cattle.

Protocol #20. When we come into our kingdom, our autocratic government will avoid ... sensibly burdening the masses of the people with taxes. ... Our rule, in which the king will enjoy the legal fiction that everything in his state belongs to him ... will be enabled to resort to the lawful confiscation of all sums of every kind for the regulation of their circulation in the state. From this it follows that taxation will best be covered by a progressive tax on property. ... Purchase, receipt of money or inheritance will be subject to the payment of a stamp progressive tax. ... Economic crises have been produced by us for the *goyim* by no other means than the withdrawal of money from circulation. ... Loans hang like a sword of Damocles over the heads of rulers, who, instead of taking from their subjects by a temporary tax, come begging with outstretched palm to our bankers.... So long as loans were internal the *goyim* only shuffled their money from the pockets of the poor to those of the rich, but when we brought up the necessary persons in order to transfer loans into the external sphere, all the wealth of states flowed into our cash boxes and all the *goyim* began to pay us the tribute of subjects.

Protocol #21. (Regarding internal loans), an exceedingly burdensome debit has been created. For the payment of interest it becomes necessary to have recourse to new loans, which do not swallow up but only add to the capital debt.... When we ascend the throne of the world all these financial and similar shifts, as being not in accord with our interests, will be swept away so as not to leave a trace, as also will be destroyed all money markets. ... We shall replace the money markets by grandiose government credit institutions.

Protocol #22. In our hands is the greatest power of our day—gold; in two days we can procure from our storehouses any quantity we may please. Surely there is no need to seek further proof that our rule is predestined by God.

Protocol #23. That the peoples may be accustomed to obedience it is necessary to inculcate lessons of humility and therefore to reduce the production of articles of luxury.... Unemployment is a most perilous thing for a government. ... Drunkeness also will be prohibited by law. Subjects...give blind obedience only to the strong hand which is absolutely independent of them. ... This Chosen One of God is chosen from above to demolish the senseless forces moved by instinct and not reason, by brutishness and not humanness.

Protocol #24. Certain members of the seed of David will prepare the kings and their heirs. ... To those persons only will be taught the practical application of the aforenamed plans by comparison of the experiences of many centuries, all the observations on the politico-economic moves and social sciences. ... Only those who are unconditionally capable for firm, even if it be to cruelty, direct rule will receive the reins of rule from our learned elders. . . . Only the king and the three who stood sponsor for him will know what is coming. . . . That the people may know and love their king, it is indispensable for him to converse in the market-places with his people. . . . The king of the Jews must not be at the mercy of his passions and especially of sensuality. . . . Our supreme lord must be of an exemplary irreproachability.

In our hands is the greatest power of our day—gold; in two days we can procure from our storehouses any quantity we may please. Surely there is no need to seek further proof that our rule is predestined by God.

The Federal Reserve building in Washington, D.C.

CHAPTER 23

The Federal Reserve System

Meyer Amschel Rothschild once said, "Let me control a nation's money and I care not who writes the laws." The power of money is so great that it leads to control of everything else.

More recently, paraphrasing the Islamic creed, Heinrich Heine said, "Money is the god of our times and Rothschild is his prophet." He was referring, of course, to the Rothschild family and to the other international bankers who control our lives.

Jews have been active in the banking business since biblical times and naturally have developed a great deal of expertise in financial matters. They created countless banks over the years, including a network of central banks in nearly every nation in the world. The Bank of Amsterdam was formed in 1609 by Jews who had been forced out of Spain in 1492. The Bank of Hamburg was created in 1619, the Bank of Sweden in 1656 and the Bank of England in 1694.

In the United States, there were periods with and without a central bank. The Bank of North America was founded in Philadelphia by Robert Morris in 1781. The first Bank of the United States was formed in 1791 by Alexander Hamilton. It had a 20-year charter which was not renewed, so it ceased to exist in 1811. The refusal to renew its charter angered British banking interests and was one of the reasons for the War of 1812.

The second Bank of the United States was formed in 1816 by Nicholas Biddle, under the direction and funding of Baron James de Rothschild. It had a 20-year charter also. President Andrew Jackson opposed the renewal of its charter, so it went out of business in 1836. The United States did not have a central bank again until 1913, when the Federal Reserve Act was passed.

The power of bankers is formidable. They can cause recessions or depressions by reducing the extension of credit and have done so on many occasions. The Panic of 1907 is an example which relates to the creation of the Federal Reserve System. As a result of that recession, Congress created a National Monetary Commission to investigate the boom and bust cycles of the economy and to recommend corrective action. Of course it was the bankers who created the panic in the first place.

Baron Alfred Rothschild of London was the mastermind behind the Federal Reserve System. He persuaded Paul Warburg of the German Reichsbank to move to America to set it up. In 1910, Warburg arranged a top secret meeting with prominent bankers at J. P. Morgan's hunting lodge on Jekyll Island, Georgia, to draft legislation and to plan how to get it passed by Congress.

Paul Warburg was then a partner in Kuhn, Loeb & Company, New York office, part of the Rothschild financial empire. The other attendees were:

Sen. Nelson Aldrich, Chairman, National Monetary Commission; Piatt Andrew, Assistant Secretary of the Treasury; Frank Vanderlip, President, National City Bank, New York; Henry P. Davidson, Senior Partner, J. P. Morgan Co.; Charles D. Norton, President, First National Bank of New York; Benjamin Strong, Partner, J. P. Morgan Co.

Two competing bills were produced—The Aldrich-Vreeland bill, which was supported by Republicans in the 1912 election year and the Owens-Glass bill, also known as the Federal Reserve

Act, which the Democrats supported. Actually both bills had similar provisions. The Aldrich-Vreeland bill never came to a vote. The Glass bill passed in the House and the Owens bill in the Senate. The differences were reconciled over a weekend in December 1913 and the final version passed on December 23, when Congress was about to adjourn for the holidays. President Wilson signed it the same day. This was the international bankers' greatest triumph of all time. It legalized the invisible government by the Money Trust.

The Federal Reserve Act provides for a system of twelve regional banks across the country, each to be capitalized by its member banks. The federal government never invested a cent in the system. It is entirely privately owned and operated. It was designed to appear to be a government agency by the creation of a Board of Governors, with an office in Washington, D.C. The governors were appointed by the president for 10 year terms (increased to 14 years in 1935) and approved by the Senate, but in practice the Federal Reserve Systems selects its own governors and the President and the Senate routinely approve them.

The system is dominated by the Federal Reserve Bank of New York, which effectively controls the nation's money supply and interest rates by means of the Federal Open Market Committee, which buys and sells securities on the open market.

The Fed can literally create money out of thin air. When the U.S. Treasury is short of money, as it always is, the Treasury asks the Fed for a loan and gives notes or bonds to secure it, which must be repaid with interest. The Fed then credits the Treasury's checking account by a computer entry, or has the Bureau of Engraving and Printing print Federal Reserve notes for use as currency. On the local level, fractional reserve banking lets the member banks make loans to their customers, also creating money out of thin air.

The principal original stockholders of the Federal Reserve Bank of New York were as follows: National City Bank, First National Bank; Marine National Bank; Chase National Bank; and the National Bank of Commerce.

These banks in turn were owned and controlled by several European banks—Rothschilds of London and Berlin, Lazard Brothers of Paris, Israel Seiff of Italy, Kuhn Loeb of Germany, the Warburgs of Amsterdam and Hamburg and by several American banks—Lehman Brothers, Goldman Sachs and the Rockefeller family. Thus the system is a private cabal, mainly owned by foreign international bankers.

Paul Warburg was one of the first governors, serving 1914-1918. He then was the representative of the Federal Reserve Bank of New York on the Federal Advisory Council for another ten years. Thus he was the dominant person on the national board from 1914 to 1928.

Also in 1913 the Sixteenth Amendment to the U. S. Constitution was supposedly approved, allowing a federal income tax. Recent studies have proved that the ratification was not valid, so the income tax remains unconstitutional. The Internal Revenue Service was created by executive order of the Secretary of the Treasury. It serves as the collection agency for the private bankers which make up the Federal Reserve System.

As planned by the bankers, the main purpose of central banks is to finance the budget deficits of the various national governments and especially to finance wars. The new Fed loaned $25 billion to the Allied nations to finance World War I. In 1917, the Fed helped finance the Russian Revolution, as well as America's entry into the war. In the 1930's they financed Hitler.

During World War I, three Jews made up a powerful triumvirate: Eugene Meyer, Chairman of the War Finance Corporation, Bernard Baruch, Chairman of the War Industries Board and Paul Warburg, Governor of the Federal Reserve Board. Louis Brandeis became a Supreme Court justice.

At the Paris Peace Conference after World War I, Baron Edmond de Rothschild served as a host. Many prominent Jews were in the American delegation, including Bernard Baruch, Albert Strauss, Walter Lippman, Felix Frankfurter, Louis Brandeis and Paul Warburg.

One of the main functions assigned to the Fed was to maintain a stable economy in order to prevent periodic recessions and depressions. In practice they did just the opposite. During the 1920's, they pursued a policy of easy money and credit which caused a speculative boom to occur. In 1929, the Fed decided to end the boom suddenly. Paul Warburg warned his friends to get out of the stock market. Many of them made a fortune by selling short. The Fed then moved $500 million of gold to Europe and tightened the rules for margin accounts on the stock market, which caused the stock market to crash. In the depression, they kept the money supply too low and restricted credit, causing the Great Depression, which was to last until World War II.

The larger the national debt becomes, the more interest the bankers earn on the money which they created out of nothing. The recent financial crisis drove the national debt to well over $10 trillion and the projected budget deficits of the next ten years will be financed mainly by more debt.

We can see how powerful the system is by observing what has happened since the Fed came into existence less than 100 years ago. In 1910, the national debt was only $1.1 billion, which figured out to $12.41 per capita. On September 30, 2008, the national debt was $10.025 trillion, or $33,237 per capita. The Treasury paid $451.2 billion in interest on this debt.

The financial crisis which began in 2008 and which was engineered by the bankers, made the situation much worse. The fiscal stimulus package and the bailouts of the large financial institutions, along with war spending, caused a budget deficit of $1.4 trillion in fiscal year 2009. The national debt amounted to 86% of our Gross Domestic Product.

In fiscal year 2010, a $1.3 trillion deficit is projected. Most of this will be funded by more debt. Congress had to increase the debt limit from $12.2 trillion to $14.3 trillion in order to be able to borrow enough to keep operating. The new limit is nearly equal to our current Gross Domestic Product of $14.5 trillion, a very unstable situation. To make matters worse, Congress passed sweeping healthcare reform, which will cost an estimated $1 trillion over the next 10 years.

The fiscal year 2011 budget calls for spending of $3.8 trillion, which will result in an estimated deficit of $1.3 trillion. Projections for the 2011-2020 fiscal years estimate a total deficit of $6.0 trillion. At some point, we will be unable to find lenders enough to support this madness and disaster will set in. This, of course, is what the international bankers had in mind right along.

We can see that Meyer Amschel Rothschild was correct in his plan to control money as the means to control the world.

The fiscal year 2011 budget calls for spending of $3.8 trillion, which will result in an estimated deficit of $1.3 trillion. Projections for the 2011-2020 fiscal years estimate a total deficit of $6 trillion. At some point, we will be unable to find lenders enough to support this madness.

CHAPTER 24

The Russian Revolution

As we saw in Chapter 19, Poland was partitioned in three phases—1772, 1793 and 1795. Much of the Pale of Settlement, where Jews were forced to live, became Russian territory. Russia became the home of about half of the Jews in the world. Most of them were descendants of the Khazars.

Jews suffered persecution in Russia for many years. The situation was made worse in 1881, when Jews assassinated Czar Alexander II. Pogroms run by the people themselves broke out.

A study done in 1886 revealed that Jews made up 4% of the Russian population, but 14% of the students at universities and 40% of the students in medical schools and law schools. Czar Alexander III was concerned that Jews were taking over the legal profession and destroying its moral standards. He decreed that no Jews would be admitted to law schools for the next 15 years.

In 1900, Russia had about 5,000,000 Jews, which was half of the world's Jewish population. Many were encouraged to emigrate to the United States.

In the Russo-Japanese War of 1904-1905, Jacob Schiff and other wealthy Jews financed Japan, which won the war even though it was a much smaller nation. During the war, a revolt led by Jews broke out, but was put down. Many of the leaders were exiled.

World War I broke out in Europe in 1914. Jews were the leaders of both the Bolshevik and Menshevik revolutionary groups. In the Spring of 1917, Czar Nicholas II was deposed and a provisional government under Kerensky set up. In October the Bolshevik Revolution took place. Russian troops were withdrawn from the battlefield and the Germans advanced toward Moscow. The Jews welcomed the Germans as liberators. By the Treaty of Brest-Litvosk in 1918, the Bolsheviks had to vacate Finland, the Baltic provinces, Poland, Ukraine and part of the Transcaucasus from Russia. These nations came under the sphere of influence of the German state.

A high percentage of the officials of the new Russian government were Jews. Among the leaders were Leon Trotsky (Lev Bronstein), Jacob Sverdlov, Lev Kamenev (Rosenfeld), Grigori Zinoviev (Hirsch Apfelbaum), Karl Radak, Maxim Litvinov (Vallatch) and Lazar Kaganovich. Vladimir Ilyich Lenin (Ulyanov) was not Jewish himself, but was of Jewish ancestry and had a Jewish wife. Joseph Stalin was an atheist, but he had three Jewish wives in succession.

The Central Committee consisted of 9 Jews and 3 others. The Executive Commission had 42 Jews and 19 others. The Council of Peoples Commissars had 17 Jews and 5 others. The Moscow Cheka (secret police) had 23 Jews and 13 others. More than 300 of the 384 Commissars were Jews. For the first time in 2,000 years, Jews were in control of a nation. The first law enacted made anti-Semitism a crime.

The Cheka, headed by Genrikh Yagoda, ran the Gulag Archipelago, a system of concentration camps which killed more than 20,000,000 prisoners in the early years of the Soviet Union and some 66,000,000 million in all. Most of the victims were Russian Orthodox Christians. This was sweet revenge for the many years of anti-Jewish pogroms in Russia.

Czar Nicholas II and his family were murdered in Ekterinburg by the Cheka. The Cathedral of St. Basil in Moscow was dynamited. There were more than 50,000 Christian churches in Russia in 1917. By the late 1930s, only 300 were left. More than 80,000 priests, monks and nuns were killed.

In the 1920s, Stalin purged most of the Jews. But he kept Lazar Kaganovich on to run the Gulag Archipelago and to starve the Ukrainians into submission. Some 9 million of them died, mostly of starvation, in the Soviet Union's main grain-producing region.

Adolf Hitler

CHAPTER 25

The Holocaust

Germany was defeated in World War I in spite of the Russian Revolution, which ended Russia's participation in the war and allowed Germany to send its troops to the western front. In 1918, Rosa Luxemberg, a Jew, led an unsuccessful Bolshevik uprising in Germany.

After the war, Germany became a federal republic with its capital at Weimar. Jews had considerable influence in the government. War reparations crippled the economy. The government started issuing paper money in ever-increasing amounts, causing massive hyperinflation in 1923.

Adolph Hitler became active in the National Socialist German Workers Party, known as the Nazi Party. He was extremely anti-Semitic. He blamed all of Germany's problems on the Jews. He used the Talmud and the *Protocols* to discredit Jews. In 1923 he led an uprising at a Munich beer hall for which he was arrested and sent to Landsberg prison. While there, he wrote his famous book, *Mein Kampf*, which outlined his plans for Germany.

The Nazi Party grew in strength over the next decade. In 1933, Hitler became Chancellor, second in power only to President Hindenburg. He envisioned a Third Reich, destined to last 1,000 years, led by the Aryan race, which he claimed to be superior to all others. He considered Jews to be less than men. He believed in a neo-pagan religion based on Norse mythology and persecuted Roman Catholics as well as Jews.

In 1933, the World Jewish Congress declared economic war on Germany. There were more than 500,000 Jews in Germany at the time. Hitler decided to drive them out of the country.

The main political opponent of the Nazi Party was the Communist Party. Many Communists were also Jews, so moving Jews out served a double purpose for Hitler.

The Reichstag building was set on fire in 1933. The Nazis blamed it on a Dutch Communist, but had actually set the fire themselves, a false flag operation, which they used as an excuse for increased government power. A series of concentration camps was set up, starting with Dachau, near Munich. In April, Hitler's SA Storm Troopers started a national boycott of Jewish businesses.

As had happened in many other lands, Jews were prosperous. Many Jews were bankers, businessmen, doctors and lawyers. Their wealth and their tendency not to assimilate with the local culture caused resentment among the Gentiles. Hitler exploited this to a degree not seen before or since.

The Nuremberg Laws were enacted in 1935. Jews were no longer allowed to hold public office. They were not permitted in cafes, places of entertainment or public baths. They could not marry or have sexual relations with non-Jews. They had to wear a yellow Star of David to identify themselves as Jews. Jewish children were humiliated in the public schools, where it was taught that "the Jew is our worst enemy." Book burnings were held.

In March 1938, Germany united with Austria. The persecution spread to that country and later to the other countries that Germany controlled.

In July 1938, President Roosevelt asked 32 nations to meet at Evian, France, to discuss resettling Jews from Germany. Little was accomplished because Jews were somewhat unpopular everywhere. Even Austria was proposed, but the Austrians did not want to admit many more Jews than they already had. Madagascar was suggested, but the French government rejected the idea. The British suggested Palestine, in furtherance of the Balfour Declaration of 1917, but the Palestinians resisted further Jewish immigration. Only the United States was receptive to admitting more Jews, but the immigration quotas allowed only a small fraction of those who wanted to come.

The worst single episode of anti-Jewish violence occurred on the night of November 9 and 10, 1938, an event called *Kristallnacht*, or "the night of broken glass." More than 190 synagogues were destroyed. Thousands of Jewish shops and homes were damaged. 35,000 Jews were arrested.

Germany and the USSR entered a non-aggression pact on August 23, 1939, agreeing not to attack each other. A week later, Germany attacked Poland in response to the Polish/Communist murder of more than 58,000 ethnic Germans in Poland, starting World War II. A few weeks later, the USSR also attacked Poland, splitting the country in two. Poland and Russia had large Jewish populations. Mass killings of Jews by German SS task forces began. The non-aggression pact did not last very long. On June 22, 1941, Germany launched Operation Barbarossa, an invasion of Russia.

A German conference was held on January 20, 1942, at Wannsee, near Berlin, to plan a final solution to the "Jewish problem." No documents remain from this conference, but we know that massive numbers of Jews were rounded up and sent in cattle cars to concentration camps in Nazi-controlled territory, mostly in Poland. Auschwitz was the most notorious of them. Jewish property was confiscated. Jews were used as slave labor at various factories which supported the German war effort. Those who were unable to work were killed.

Historians disagree as to the extent of the horrors committed at these concentration camps. The report of the International Committee of the Red Cross is vastly at odds with the official version of the Holocaust. The Red Cross estimated that 500,000 Jews died of various causes in the camps, as compared to the official claim of 6,000,000. But nearly everyone agrees that there was a vast network of camps with forced labor throughout Nazi-controlled territory, that many died of typhus and other diseases and that malnutrition was involved, especially late in the war years.

It is unfortunate that the official story contains errors and exaggerations, because these things reduce the credibility of the whole story. The basic facts are more than enough to support the case against the Nazis. Killing even one person for his religious beliefs is one too many. The indignities heaped on German Jews before the war began were a cause of international revulsion. Taking people forcibly from their homes, confiscating their property, transporting them to distant camps and forcing them to do slave labor was totally unacceptable.

Of course when the shoe was on the other foot and Jews were in control of Russia and the Soviet Union, they managed to kill more than 20 million Christians during the period when they ran the gulag concentration camps and another 10 million in the Ukraine. Let that serve as a warning of what will happen if Jews get control of the whole world.

The report of the International Committee of the Red Cross is vastly at odds with the official version of the Holocaust. The Red Cross estimated that 500,000 Jews died of various causes in the camps, as compared to the official claim of 6,000,000.

THE BOMBING OF THE KING DAVID HOTEL

CHAPTER 26

The State of Israel

As we saw in Chapter 21, the Balfour Declaration in 1917 promised Great Britain's support for a Jewish homeland in Palestine, which was then part of the Ottoman Empire. It did not become a British Mandate until 1922.

Palestine is a relatively small country, about the size of the state of Massachusetts. In 1920, it was inhabited by about 800,000 Arab Muslims and Christians and a few other groups. The *Yishuv*, the Jewish community in Palestine, was very small. Jews immigrated there in small numbers after 1917, sometimes clashing with the Palestinians.

When Hitler came to power in Nazi Germany in 1933, Jews were severely persecuted. Lord Rothschild and the Zionists negotiated the *ha'avara*, a transfer agreement with Hitler which allowed the transfer of some Jewish assets to Palestine along with the emigration of Jews. Between 1933 and 1939, about 235,000 Jews left Germany for Palestine.

As the number of Jews increased in Palestine, conflicts with the Palestinians became more frequent. In 1936, the Arabs staged a general strike. The British government put severe restrictions on further Jewish migration.

The Zionists set up Haganah as their official underground military force. During World War II, this group was secretly armed.

The increasing hostility led to the formation of two terrorist groups—Irgun Zvai Leumi, the National Military Organization led by Menachem Begin and the LEHI, Fighters for the Freedom of Israel, or Stern Gang, led by Abraham Stern.

In 1944, there were about 1 million Arabs in Palestine, 136,000 of whom were Christians. There were about 528,000 Jews. Lord Rothschild purchased land from Arab owners. Jewish-owned banks also made mortgage loans to Arabs and foreclosed on them if the loans defaulted.

In 1946, the Zionists initiated terrorist activities. The Irgun Zvai Leumi blew up the King David Hotel, where the British military headquarters were located. After that, 100,000 European Jews were allowed to immigrate to Palestine. The Stern Gang killed Lord Moyne (Walter Guinness), the British executive in Palestine.

In 1947, the United Nations partitioned Palestine. Jews were allocated 56% of the land and the native Palestinians 44%. The Palestinians revolted.

On April 9, 1948, Haganah troops attacked the Palestinian village of Deir Yassin and massacred all 250 inhabitants. This was in accordance with the ancient practice of *cherem*, the annihilation of enemy lands and peoples. During the next few years, some 700,000 Palestinian Arabs fled to surrounding Arab nations in fear of their lives, leaving only about 160,000 in Palestine.

On May 14, 1948, the State of Israel was proclaimed, fulfilling the initial Zionist objective of a Jewish homeland. This, of course, was just the first step toward *Eretz Israel*, a Greater Israel extending from the Nile to the Euphrates and rule of the world from Jerusalem. David Ben-Gurion was the first Prime Minister and Dr. Chaim Weizmann the first president.

Israel's Arab neighbors—Egypt, Transjordan, Syria, Iraq and Lebanon—then joined forces and attacked the new nation. The War of Independence lasted for two years, 1948-1949. The Israel

Defense Forces, with considerable military and economic help from the United States, won the war, but Transjordan (now called Jordan) annexed the West Bank.

During the course of the war, in September 1948, the Stern Gang assassinated the United Nations mediator, Count Folke Bernadotte.

In 1950, the Law of Return was passed by the Knesset. It gives every Jew in the world the right to settle in Israel and provides that no Palestinians can become citizens of Israel.

In 1955, Defense Minister Pinhas Lavon staged terrorist bombings to undermine Egypt's relations with the West. On February 28, Israel attacked an Egyptian army base in Gaza and began a campaign against Egypt in the Sinai.

In July 1956, President Nasser of Egypt nationalized the Suez Canal. On October 29, Israel invaded Egypt. Great Britain and France followed two days later. The United States opposed these actions and demanded that Israel withdraw.

In 1964, Israel's National Water Carrier diverted water from the Jordan River. The Arab League formed the Palestine Liberation Organization, headed by Yasser Arafat.

The Six Day War occurred in 1967. Levi Eshkol was Prime Minister and Moshe Dayan Defense Minister. On June 5, Israel launched air attacks on air fields in Egypt, Syria, Jordan and Iraq. Israel captured the Sinai from Egypt, East Jerusalem and the West Bank from Jordan and the Golan Heights from Syria. The Soviet Union severed diplomatic relations with Israel.

A serious incident occurred during this war. The *USS Liberty*, an electronic surveillance ship, was patrolling in international waters in the Mediterranean, north of Egypt. Israel resented the presence of a spy ship in the area and sent aircraft, gunboats and torpedo boats to destroy it. Some 34 of the crew were killed and 171 wounded, but miraculously the *USS Liberty* remained afloat. The power of the Israeli lobby over Washington was already so great that President Lyndon Johnson ordered the recall of U. S. fighters from an aircraft carrier in the area and the cover-up of the whole incident. Admiral John McCain Jr., father of the U.S. senator, ordered the crew to keep their mouths shut about the whole event. Israel claimed that it was a case of mistaken identity of the ship, believing it to be Egyptian.

After the Six Day War, the Soviet Union helped rebuild the Arab military forces. From 1968 to 1970, Israel had a series of clashes with Egypt along the Suez Canal.

The Yom Kippur War occurred in 1973. This time the Arab nations of Egypt and Syria attacked Israel on the high holy day of Yom Kippur, which fell on October 6 that year. Israel was largely unprepared for the attack and was nearly defeated. A massive airlift of war materiel from the United States saved the nation. On October 7, 1973, Senator J. William Fulbright stated, "The Israelis control the policy in the Congress and the Senate." The Arab nations retaliated against the United States with the OPEC oil embargo, which caused the price of crude oil to quadruple and caused massive oil shortages and long lines at gasoline stations across the country.

In 1974, Prime Minister Golda Meir was criticized for the lack of preparedness in the war and was replaced by Yitzhak Rabin of the Labor Party.

In 1976, Israel demonstrated its military ability by a brilliant raid on the airport at Entebbe, Uganda, to recover hostages held there.

In 1977, Menachem Begin of the right-wing Likud Party became Prime Minister.

The Camp David Accords, sponsored by President Jimmy Carter, were signed by Israel and Egypt in 1979. Israel agreed to return the Sinai to Egypt in exchange for peace.

In 1981, Israel destroyed Iraq's nuclear facility at Osirak.

On June 6, 1982, Israel attacked Lebanon to eliminate the

THE STATE OF ISRAEL

Palestinian military presence in southern Lebanon. The attack was especially brutal. Cluster bombs were used on civilian targets. Schools, hospitals and apartment buildings were bombed. Refugees at camps in Sabra and Chatila were butchered. The brutality was so extreme that there were anti-war demonstrations in Tel Aviv.

In 1983, Yitzhak Shamir became Prime Minister. He was succeeded in 1984 by Shimon Peres of the Labor Party. Shamir again became Prime Minister in 1986.

An *intifada* uprising broke out in December 1987. Yitzhak Rabin, now Defense Minister, set an "iron fist" policy to suppress it. It lasted until 1991.

The Persian Gulf War broke out in 1991. It was a major effort by United States military forces and their allies. Israel did not participate.

Yitzhak Rabin again became Prime Minister in 1992. In 1993, he and Yasser Arafat of the PLO signed the Oslo Accords for peace between Israel and the PLO. Hard liners in Israel considered Rabin to be a traitor. In 1995 he was assassinated.

Benjamin Netanyahu of the Likud Party became Prime Minister in 1996 and served in that office until 1999.

A second *intifada* broke out in 2000 and lasted until 2003.

On October 3, 2001, Prime Minister Ariel Sharon made an interesting comment to his cabinet. He said, "We, the Jewish people, control America and the Americans know it." This is undoubtedly true. No American politician dares to speak against Israel. Over the years, American economic and military aid to Israel has exceeded $1 trillion. We will expand on this theme in later chapters.

In 2002, Israel occupied the West Bank. More development projects were begun. Jews now control 78% of the land, up from the original 56%. Soon they will "own" it all.

In the summer of 2006, Israel again attacked Lebanon, which

housed Hezbollah forces.

In 2007, Hamas won the elections in Gaza. Israel invaded Gaza in September and has held its 1,500,000 Palestinian residents captive ever since. In July 2009, Amnesty International condemned Israel for total disregard of international law and human life in Gaza.

In April 2009, Benjamin Netanyahu returned as Prime Minister, promising a continuation of hard line policy.

In summary, Israel has experienced violence nearly continuously ever since its creation in 1948 and even before it became a nation. Given the Zionist policy for world conquest and the expansion of Israel itself from the Nile to the Euphrates, the violence is bound to continue. Israel is pressing for an attack on Iran, which will undoubtedly lead to World War III.

If Israel's existence is threatened by war, it threatens to use the "Samson Option." It has more than 400 nuclear warheads and enough missiles to destroy every major city in Europe, from London to Moscow. As in the case of Samson bringing down the Philistine temple with his own death, Israel will not die alone. The battle of Armageddon may be at hand.

Israel has more than 400 nuclear warheads and enough missiles to destroy every major city in Europe. As in the case of Samson bringing down the Philistine temple with his own death, Israel will not die alone.

The Frankfurt School

CHAPTER 27

Gaining Control of American Culture

The Zionist goal of world domination requires gaining control of every nation in the world, preferably by subtle means which win the hearts and minds of the people. They have learned the importance of keeping a low profile, using people and organizations to front for them and keeping the Jewish leadership behind the scenes as much as possible.

Their methods come from many sources, including the Rothschild protocols, the Order of Illuminati, the Communist Manifesto, the *Protocols of the Learned Elders of Zion* and the Humanist Manifesto. In keeping with the dictum that the end justifies the means, they use any techniques necessary to achieve their goal, including propaganda, disinformation, deception, secrecy, espionage, blackmail and physical force.

Jews have always been among the leaders of change and even of revolutions, over the centuries. Most people prefer stability and are resentful of change, especially rapid change. That is one of the reasons that Jews are often disliked by the *goyim* and become the victims of oppression. Yet that very anti-Semitism helps to keep them united in their fight for world supremacy.

One of the key planks in the Communist Manifesto was free public education for all children. This allows Jews to control the information going into the impressionable minds of the young.

If they can get to the children by the time they are age seven, they have them for life.

In the colonial period of America and in the early years of the republic, home schooling was the principal means of educating the young, although there were a number of private schools available to the more affluent. Public schools were almost non-existent before 1850, but after 1870 they became fairly common. This was partly because the Jewish population in America increased rapidly during this time, from about 230,000 in 1870 to 4,500,000 in 1926.

Citing the Communist Manifesto as the source of the idea for public schools would have gained very little support. Even calling it a Socialist idea would not help much. So the concept was labeled as Liberal or Progressive and it was widely accepted.

Another concept which helped the Jewish cause was secular humanism, which held that religion is irrelevant in modern society, God is dead and man can take over where God left off—if there ever *was* a God.

John Dewey was an early leader in the public education system. He was an advocate of progressive education, liberalism and secular humanism. His idea was to indoctrinate the children into becoming faithful servants of the secular rulers. More recently, Jews have focused on getting control of local school boards and determining the curriculum which is taught to the students and control of the National Education Association, the teachers' main union. Anything to do with Christianity has been removed from the public schools.

Other Jewish ideas found their way into American law. Starting about 1870, Harvard Law School started teaching that the Constitution was an evolving document, subject to differing interpretations as time went on. The writings of the founding fathers who wrote the Constitution were not considered particularly relevant. Case law and the opinions of contemporary

Supreme Court Justices, were far more important. The process was similar to the development of the Talmud, which expresses the opinions of the rabbis and often leads to mutually contradictory laws which add confusion to the situation, which is one of the goals of the *Protocols*. The idea is to sow confusion by conflicting ideas in order to wear everyone out.

The field of psychology is another idea invented by Jews. Sigmund Freud, Karl Jung and Abraham Maslow were the early pioneers. Jews are still prominent in psychology to this day.

Many of the Jews who immigrated to America settled in New York, where they developed considerable political power. They formed the Kehillah, which took over control of Tammany Hall. Today about one third of the Jews in the world live in the United States, many of them in New York City.

Another Jewish invention was the Institute for Social Research, also known as the Frankfurt School, which was organized in 1923 in Frankfurt, Germany, to promote the plan for world domination by gaining control of the culture of the nations. They were influenced by the writings of the Italian Communist, Antonio Gramsci. They developed critical theory to destroy Western culture—bringing existing society down by means of unremitting destructive criticism. When Hitler came to power in Germany, the school moved to New York and changed its name to the New School for Social Research. Its members included many people in the social sciences, such as Eric Fromm in psychology, Herbert Marcuse in political science and Franz Boas in anthropology.

One of the lasting effects of cultural Communism is political correctness.

A vital aspect of culture control is the media, by which the public gets most of its information about the world. Naturally Jews put a great deal of emphasis on controlling the information which reaches the public. Their control of the newspapers goes back more than a century. They gradually took control of radio, television, theater, movies, magazines, book publishing, school books and the recording industry. Their control is not absolute, of course and there still are alternative sources of information, especially the Internet. Nevertheless, the vast majority of people hear only what Jews want them to hear.

Jews control many of the large foundations, which in turn give financial grants to favored individuals, think tanks and other organizations. By this means they have indirect control of colleges and universities and promote publications and research helpful to their cause. They have also set up a network of students who report on their professors who do not follow their party line.

The Anti-Defamation League of B'nai B'rith was founded in 1913 to combat anti-Semitism. This has become a very large organization over the years. It monitors public officials, news media, organizations and individuals who are critical of Judaism, Israel, Zionism, or anything else related to their cause. It works with the FBI, CIA, Mossad and police forces as an unofficial secret police force. It has developed a blacklist with over 500,000 names.

For many years, Jews have supported the Civil Rights movement in a Black-Jewish alliance. The National Association for the Advancement of Colored People was formed in New York in 1909. The entire national board of directors were Jews. Blacks were used as front men. Blacks who opposed the party line, such as Booker T. Washington and Marcus Garvey, were ousted. They also funded the Southern Christian Leadership Conference of Dr. Martin Luther King, Jr., the Congress of Racial Equality of James Farmer and the Student Nonviolent Coordinating Committee of Stokely Carmichael.

Jews are very active in the Women's Liberation movement. Gloria Steinem, Betty Friedan and Bella Abzug were among the leaders. Other well-known Jewish feminists include Joyce Brothers, Ann Landers, Abigail Van Buren (Dear Abby) and Laura Schlessinger.

Jews were also active in the Marxist-oriented Yippie Movement, led by Jerry Rubin and Abbie Hoffman.

Jewish influence in politics is enormous, especially at the national level. They typically supply about 80% of the campaign funds of Democratic candidates and 50% of the funds of Republican candidates. Furthermore, they control the press. Presidential candidates must appear before the America Israel Public Affairs Committee and promise total support for Israel in order to get their support.

One of the best ways to weaken a country is to encourage the break-up of the family unit. To this end, Jews support secular humanism, interracial marriages, abortion, gay rights, same-sex marriages and sexual liberation. They support child protective services, which allow children to be taken from their parents for a variety of reasons. They encourage the scheduling of sport games and practices at dinner times so that families rarely eat together and on Sundays so the children can't go to Sunday school.

Jewish influence sometimes extends to seemingly unlikely situations. For example, during World War II, General George Patton was one of our most effective generals, but he criticized the conspiracy of international bankers, labor leaders, Jews and Communists. Jews forced his dismissal as head of the Third Army.

William F. Buckley was a Roman Catholic who served as a front man for the neo-conservatives. He published *National Review* magazine and hosted the television show, *Firing Line*. He was billed as a conservative, but he attacked many conservatives, such as Father Coughlin, Ayn Rand, Joe Sobran, Pat Buchanan, Sam Francis and the John Birch Society. He had many Jewish friends, including Irving Kristol, the founder of the neo-conservative movement and his son, William Kristol, publisher of the *Weekly Standard*.

Jews are prominent in virtually every aspect of American culture. For example, in the 1960's, folk music was used with revolutionary lyrics to promote their cause. Among the Jewish singers were Rambling Jack Elliott, Woody Guthrie, Bob Dylan, Pete Seeger, Joan Baez and the trio Peter, Paul and Mary.

Famous Jewish song writers include Irving Berlin, Jerome Kern, George Gershwin, Richard Rodgers and Barry Manilow.

In classical music, Jewish composers include Aaron Copland and Leonard Bernstein. Many of the musicians and conductors of symphony orchestras are Jewish.

Famous Jewish movie actors include Sammy Davis Jr. (a black convert to Judaism), Mel Brooks, John Garfield and Barbra Streisand.

Famous Jewish authors include Saul Bellow, Arthur Miller, Philip Roth, J. D. Salinger, Norman Mailer, Herman Wouk, Alan Ginsberg, Lionel Trilling and Ayn Rand.

There are many well-known Jewish comedians, including Henny Youngman, the Marx brothers, Eddie Cantor, Al Jolsen, Fannie Brice, Woody Allen, Lenny Bruce, Mike Nichols and Jerry Seinfeld.

In summary, although America remains nominally a predominantly Christian nation, Jews have managed to get their ideas across to the vast majority of Americans. One could fairly say that America has become Jewish in its outlook.

The Zionist goal of world domination requires gaining control of every nation in the world, preferably by subtle means which win the hearts and minds of the people.

J.P. Morgan: Rothschild frontman

CHAPTER 28

The Media

One of the most vital parts of the Jewish plan for world conquest is control of the media, which allows them to control the information that reaches the public. Words are far more important than guns when it comes to winning the hearts and minds of people.

In 1848, at the Jewish Conference in Krakow, Jews determined to become the owners of the most powerful newspapers in Europe. In 1915, a group surrounding Rothschild front man J.P. Morgan did the same thing in America, buying the editorial policy of the 25 largest newspapers. They later took control of radio, television, movies and all other forms of media.

Most of the news in America, whether in newspapers, radio, or television, originates with Associated Press. Jonathan Wolman is the executive editor and Michael Silverman is the managing editor of Associated Press, which is controlled by Reuters, which in turn is controlled by the Rothschilds. Thus Jews are able to put their spin on the news and to control what is published.

Today Jews run the major magazines: *Time, Newsweek* and *U.S. News and World Report*. They run the major newspapers, including the *New York Times, Wall Street Journal* and *Washington Post*. They also control the major television networks: NBC, CBS and ABC. Since the vast majority of Americans get their news from one or more of these sources, the Jewish point of view is all most people hear.

Control of the news is only part of the story. Jewish control of the media extends to entertainment, book publishing, school textbooks, movies and recordings.

Interlocking directorates are quite common in the media industry. Officers and directors of one firm also sit on the board of other firms.

The media barons are mostly pro-Zionist and most are Jewish. They work with bankers, corporate bosses and government officials. In addition to the owners and top executives, many Jews are in supporting positions which allow them to control the scripts which the newscasters deliver to the public.

Much of the media is owned by conglomerates. The largest of these in terms of revenue is Time Warner, which was acquired by AOL in 2000 but kept its original name. It is headed by Gerald Levin. Among its holdings are Time, Inc., Turner Broadcasting, HBO, CNN, Cinemax, Warner Brothers, Warner Music, Castle Rock and the magazines *Sports Illustrated*, *People*, *Money* and *Fortune*.

Walt Disney Company, headed by Michael Eisner (Jewish), owns Walt Disney Pictures, Touchstone TV, Buena Vista TV, Touchstone Pictures, Miramax Films and Capital Cities/ABC Inc, which owns ABC and 10 other TV stations, 54 radio stations, ESPN, the Disney Channel, A&E, Lifetime TV, the History Channel, 20 magazines and several book publishers.

Viacom, run by Sumner Redstone, owns CBS and 38 other TV stations, 185 radio stations, Paramount Pictures, Country Music TV, Nashville Network, Showtime, MTV, Black Entertainment TV, the Movie Channel, Simon & Schuster, Scribner, Pocket Books, Blockbuster stores, theme parks and video games.

General Electric Company is the parent company of NBC Universal, of which it owns 80% and Vivendi 20%. NBC Universal owns NBC, CNBC, MSNBC, Bravo, Universal Studios, NBC Entertainment, USA Networks and Interscope Records.

The News Corporation, owned by Rupert Murdoch, who is

not Jewish but is a devoted Zionist, owns Fox TV, Fox News, 20th Century Fox Films, Harper Collins, Direct TV, *TV Guide*, *New York Post*, *Wall Street Journal* and *Weekly Standard*.

Jewish control is not absolute, of course. There are hundreds of independent radio stations and talk show hosts, magazines and newspapers, but so far they reach a relatively small segment of the population.

More important is the Internet, which no one controls and which is used by many millions of people. As public outrage about the recent activities of the federal government is reaching critical proportions, that medium could reverse many of the Jewish gains.

CHAPTER 29

Attacks on the Vatican

The recent attacks on the Vatican and criticism of Pope Benedict XVI are just the latest of a long series of Jewish attacks on its arch-enemy, the Roman Catholic Church. The Church has always been deemed anti-Semitic by the Jews, particularly regarding the issue of the crucifixion of Jesus. Now that Jews control the media, they are using it to get even.

In previous chapters, we discussed some of the forms of earlier Jewish opposition to the Church. The Babylonian Talmud, written about A.D. 500 and revised many times ever since, contains many anti-Christian passages. Kabbalah was introduced to Pope Sixtus IV, who ruled 1471-1484, by Pico della Mirandola and to Pope Leo X, who ruled 1514-1521, by Johannes Reuchlin.

Jews supported the Protestant Reformation, which began in 1517 and the formation of the Rosicrucians in 1579. They established Freemasonry as a means of furthering their goal of world rule in 1650, with only the highest ranking members being informed that their god was Lucifer.

Jewish plans were set forth in Mayer Amschel Rothschild's protocols of 1773, the Order of Illuminati formed in 1776 and the *Protocols of the Learned Elders of Zion* in 1897. We also saw how Jews founded Communism in 1848 and Zionism in 1897.

The Congress of Vienna in 1815, concluding the Napoleonic

Wars, brought emancipation to Jews in Europe. No longer were they confined to ghettoes. In 1869 they held a synod in Leipzig, where they emphasized modernist principles and the rights of man for Jews to divest themselves of their governments with absolute civil liberty and equality with Christians. Jews soon took over everything—gold, businesses, the stock market, political appointments, education, the press and so on.

In the Italian Revolution of 1870, Jews supported Freemasons, Mazzini, Garibaldi and Cavour. Rome was conquered. Pope Pius IX was made a prisoner. Italy was unified for the first time in recent history.

Modernism gradually took hold in Europe and the United States, particularly in the 20th century and was a direct challenge to the conservatism of the Roman Catholic Church. Pope Pius X (ruled 1903-1914) was especially opposed to modernism. He was canonized in 1954 by Pope Pius XII and had the Society of St. Pius X named after him, formed by Archbishop Marcel Lefebvre in 1970. In 1904, Pope Pius X told Theodor Herzl, the Zionist leader, that since Jews have not recognized Jesus as Lord, so Christians cannot recognize the Jewish people or a Jewish homeland in Palestine.

In 1929, Pope Pius XI and Benito Mussolini agreed to the Lateran Treaty. The Church agreed to recognize the Republic of Italy, which had been formed as a result of the Italian Revolution of 1870 and Italy recognized the sovereignty of Vatican City as a separate state, tiny though it was, within the borders of the city of Rome.

In the 1930s, about 1,100 Communist Party members infiltrated the Roman Catholic Church. They became priests. Some of them went on to become bishops and even cardinals. They were a source of support for liberal, modernist ideas.

In 1933, Pope Pius XI signed a concordat with Hitler and Germany, but after Nazi repression of the Jews and Catholics became oppressive, he denounced it in 1937.

The Vatican Information Service was formed in 1944. It engages in intelligence activities.

In 1961, Pope John XXIII met with Jules Isaac, a French Jew, who stated that the Church had preached anti-Semitism for 2000 years. The Pope, who sympathized with the modernists, called the Second Vatican Council, better known as Vatican II, which met in three phases in 1962-1965.

Its primary purpose was *aggiornamento*—bringing the Church up to date with the modern world. The first session opened in 1962, the second in 1963 and the third in 1964. There was heavy Jewish lobbying. Malachi Martin, a liberal Irish Jesuit and an assistant to Cardinal Bea, acted as a lobbyist for the Jews and was paid by the American Jewish Committee.

Cardinal Augustin Bea, a German Jesuit and head of the Vatican Secretariat for the Promotion of Christian Unity, met in New York in 1963 with Rabbi Abraham Heschel and the AJC. He drafted a Jewish Declaration about improving Catholic-Jewish relations. This ultimately became *Nostra Aetate*, "Declaration on the Relation of the Church to Non-Christian Religions," which deplored anti-Semitism and declared the obvious, that only the Jewish leaders of the day, not all Jews, were responsible for the death of Jesus and that modern Jews had nothing to do with it.

On the other side of the modernity issue, Cardinal Alfredo Ottavini, Prefect of the Holy Office, drafted documents to oppose modernity and to preserve Christian morality from corrupting influences, such as sexuality, psychoanalysis and Communism.

Pope John XXIII died in 1963. Cardinal Giovani Montini, the Archbishop of Milan, was elected to succeed him. He chose the name Pope Paul VI. He traveled extensively, both as cardinal and pope. He continued the work of Vatican II and ruled from 1963 to 1978.

French Archbishop Marcel Lefebvre was a conservative. He confronted Cardinal Joseph Ratzinger, who became Pope Benedict XVI in 1995, at Vatican II. He advocated the kingship of Christ versus modernism. He founded the Society of St. Pius X in 1970. He consecrated four bishops in 1989 without Vatican approval. They were excommunicated by Pope John Paul II, but later reinstated by Pope Benedict XVI.

In 1966, the American Jewish Congress threatened to boycott the Passion Play at Oberammergau because of its anti-Semitic message about the death of Jesus. The play had a long history. The inhabitants of that village had made a promise to God in 1633 that they would perform the play every ten years if he would save them from the plague. Using the authority of Vatican II, Jews got the village to tone down the part about the Jewish involvement and in later years got even more concessions.

In 1973, Pope Paul VI met with Prime Minister Golda Meir of Israel. He disapproved of Israel's ruthlessness to the Palestinians. Later that year he met with President Richard Nixon and told of his disapproval of the war in Vietnam.

In 1978, John Paul I died after only 33 days as pope. The official cause was listed as a heart attack, but many believe he was poisoned for investigating irregularities of the Vatican bank, which was involved in money laundering connected to the drug trade. This would have exposed the Propaganda Two Masonic Lodge, the Central Intelligence Agency, the international bankers and ultimately the Jewish connection.

In 1981, Pope John Paul II, who had more liberal leanings that his predecessors, was shot in St. Peter's Square by Mehemet Ali Agca, but survived. He later forgave the assailant. It was suspected that Iranian fundamentalists were behind the attack.

In 1986, Pope John Paul II said in the Great Synagogue of Rome, "Jews are our dearly beloved brothers; in a certain way, indeed . . . our elder brothers in the faith." You can imagine how grateful Jews were to hear these words from the leader of their ancient adversary.

ATTACKS ON THE VATICAN

In 1993, during the pontificate of this same gentleman, the Vatican granted full diplomatic recognition to the State of Israel. In April 2005, Pope John Paul II died. He was succeeded by Cardinal Joseph Ratzinger, a native of Germany and head of the Congregation of the Doctrine of the Faith. He opposed the socially permissive ways of Europe and modernism. He took the name Pope Benedict XVI. The rest of this chapter will discuss his pontificate to date, a period of five years so far.

Jews realized at the outset that the new pope needed to be watched carefully. He came from Germany, the headquarters of the Holocaust. He had been a member of Hitler Youth and the German Army. He had been Archbishop of Munich, the city where Nazism started. And of course he was described as being very conservative and opposed to liberal modernism.

On November 6, 2007, Pope Benedict XVI welcomed King Abdullah of Saudi Arabia to the Vatican. He sought common ground with the Muslims and apologized for an earlier remark about the warlike behavior of Islam.

On February 23, 2008, he eased restrictions on the use of the Tridentine Latin mass which Vatican II had put in place to encourage the use of local languages in place of Latin in the mass.

He visited the United States in April 2008 for six days. He had two meetings with Jewish leaders during his stay, including a visit to the Park Avenue East Synagogue in New York City.

On January 25, 2009, he reinstated the four conservative bishops who had been excommunicated by Pope John Paul II. One of them was Bishop Richard Williamson, who had made public statements questioning the facts of the Holocaust. For example, he claimed that fewer than 300,000 Jews had perished, rather than 6,000,000.

On February 10, 2009, the selling of indulgences was re-established. This was one of the abuses which Martin Luther had complained about in 1517.

On February 18, the pope met with a delegation from the Council of Presidents of Major Jewish Organizations. He made plans to visit Israel, show up at Holocaust memorial shrines and called "Holocaust denial" a crime against God.

He visited Israel on May 11, 2009. While there, he was criticized for having been a member of Hitler Youth and the German army. Pope Pius XII was also criticized for not having done enough to save Jews during the Holocaust.

On July 7, he issued his Charity in Truth encyclical, recommending world government to oversee the economy and tend to the needs of the poor.

On October 21, 2009, Cardinal William Levada, Prefect of the Congregation for the Doctrine of the Faith, invited conservative Anglicans who were unhappy about the ordination of female priests and gay bishops to join the Roman Catholic Church.

On December 20, 2009, the pope confirmed the virtues of Pope John Paul II and Pope Pius XII, moving them a step closer to beatification and sainthood. Jews approved of the advancement of Pope John Paul II, but objected to that of Pope Pius XII for his lack of sufficient action during the Holocaust.

On January 12, 2010, the pope met with the Jewish community at the Great Synagogue of Rome, as Pope John Paul II had done in 1986.

In summary, there were pluses and minuses in the pope's actions, from the Jewish point of view. In March 2010 Jews began a series of articles, accusing him of covering up the abuse of children by priests while he was Archbishop of Munich. They called for his resignation. It will be interesting to see how all this plays out.

The recent attacks on the Vatican and criticism of Pope Benedict XVI are just the latest of a long series of Jewish attacks on its arch-enemy, the Roman Catholic Church.

CHAPTER 30

Espionage

From Biblical times, Jews have made a specialty of espionage and intelligence activities. Ever since the Assyrians captured Samaria in 722 B.C. and drove the ten northern tribes out of Israel, starting the diaspora, Jews have had to maintain written contact with each other in order to maintain their unity. They found it necessary to share information on matters relating to business, politics and military activities. In many cases, they used their knowledge to obtain positions of power in the nations in which they lived as minorities.

Jews have also used their espionage skills against their arch enemy, the Roman Catholic Church. For example, in England, in the aftermath of King Henry VIII's declaring himself the head of the Church in England, there was a lengthy period of conflict between Catholics and Protestants. Jews supplied espionage resources to the Protestants, including Sir Francis Walsingham, the head of intelligence for Queen Elizabeth I.

As Jews got more and more involved in international banking, their intelligence operations grew apace. One notable result of this activity was the financial killing which Nathan Rothschild made as a result of knowledge of Napoleon's defeat at Waterloo a day before the news became general knowledge.

In more recent times, Jews were instrumental in organizing MI-5, the Security Service and MI-6, the Secret Intelligence Service, in the United Kingdom in 1909, shortly before World War I broke out. Jews occupy many positions in these agencies today.

After the Bolshevik Revolution in Russia in 1917, Jews controlled the government, including the Cheka, the secret police. They were active in Soviet and Russian intelligence in its various organizations—OGPU, NKVD, MGB, KGB and now the FSB and SVR.

William Wiseman was one of the members of "The Room," an early intelligence organization in the United States, which also included Vincent Astor, Allen Dulles, William Donovan and others.

During World War II, MI-6 helped organize the Office of Strategic Services in 1941. This group was headed mostly by Ivy League WASP's, but many Jews were included in the ranks. After the war, President Truman disbanded the OSS and replaced it with the Central Intelligence Group in 1946.

In 1946, the United Kingdom-United States Communications Intelligence Agreement was reached, which also included Canada, Australia and New Zealand. It set up a number of listening stations around the world to monitor radio traffic. Today it runs the Echelon program, which monitors all telephone, facsimile and Internet messages worldwide.

The National Security Act of 1947 consolidated the American armed forces into the National Military Establishment, later renamed the Department of Defense. It also established the National Security Council and the Central Intelligence Agency (CIA).

The primary mission of the CIA was to coordinate the efforts of the various elements of the intelligence community and to make a daily summary report to the president. Its Directorate of Intelligence is staffed by a large number of people with PhD degrees, but historically they have been hampered by not receiving enough human intelligence to make accurate intelligence assessments. Many key events have not been predicted over the years.

The other main component of the CIA and the one which has

been given the most funding, has been known by several names, but has always been involved in clandestine operations and espionage. The Office of Special Projects was formed within the National Security Council to conduct covert operations and the Office of Policy Coordination to conduct political action, black propaganda and paramilitary operations. In 1952, these groups were merged into the CIA as the Directorate of Plans. In 1973, it was renamed the Directorate of Operations and more recently the National Clandestine Service.

Right from the start, the CIA has been involved in black operations not contemplated in its original statutory authority. In 1947, it was involved in covert paramilitary operations in Greece and the following year in Italy, the Philippines and Thailand. It worked with MI-6 in Operation Apple Pie to recruit former Nazi Gestapo members for use as spies. It ran Operation Mockingbird, the infiltration of the major news media, Operation Octopus, electronic surveillance in the United States and Operation Orwell, the surveillance of American political and religious leaders.

Almost everything the CIA does is classified top secret in order to protect "national security." In reality, many foreign nations have a pretty good idea of what the CIA is up to. The main purpose of the secrecy is to keep the American public unaware of the atrocities being committed by their own government.

In 1950, the CIA set up its International Organizations Division to support left-wing non-Communist organizations. The Congress of Cultural Freedom was part of this.

Israel created its foreign intelligence agency, Mossad, in 1951. It is a relatively small group and it relies on volunteers in foreign nations to provide logistical support, such as housing, transportation and supplies. In the United States, for example, there are about 10,000 *sayanim* (helpers) assisting Mossad. Israel also has an internal security service, Shin Bet, as well as military intelligence units. Mossad also works with various Jewish organizations in the United States, such as the Jewish Defense League and the Anti-Defamation League.

From 1951 to 1953, the CIA worked with MI-6 on Operation Ajax, ousting Prime Minister Mohammed Mossadegh of Iran, who had nationalized the Anglo-Iranian Oil Company.

In 1952, the National Security Agency was created. It was put in charge of developing cryptographic systems for the United States and with breaking the codes of foreign nations. Today it also runs a vast surveillance network.

In 1953, as a result of the Korean War, the CIA began MK/ULTRA, a long-term series of mind control experiments involving LSD and other drugs.

In 1954, after the French were defeated in Indochina, the CIA took over operations in Vietnam, including the French drug trade. The CIA was in charge of operations there from 1954 to 1965, when the military took over and again from 1973 to 1975 after the military left.

Also in 1954, the CIA entered an intelligence sharing agreement with Israel's Mossad. Jews have long been part of the Soviet intelligence apparatus, which the CIA has been largely unable to penetrate. Internally, the CIA entered the Rogers-Houston Memorandum, whereby the Department of Justice agreed not to prosecute CIA people engaged in covert operations. And James Jesus Angleton, a Roman Catholic, Zionist and Skull and Bones member, was made head of the Counterintelligence Staff.

In 1955, the CIA began Operation Lingual, in which it opened mail between the United States and the Soviet Union.

In 1959, Civil Air Transport, which the OSS had originated in World War II in support of the Chinese drug trade, was renamed Air America, a CIA proprietary airline which grew to over 12,000 employees. Its counterpart in the Latin American drug trade, Southern Air Transport, was formed a year later.

In 1961, an attempted invasion of Cuba failed in a disaster

known as the Bay of Pigs. The CIA set up Operation Mongoose, the purpose of which was to assassinate Fidel Castro. A number of attempts were made on his life, all of them unsuccessful.

The Defense Intelligence Agency was set up in 1961 to coordinate the intelligence activities of the Army, Navy, Air Force and Marine Corps. A year later, the National Reconnaissance Office was formed.

In 1963, Secretary of Defense Robert McNamara commissioned the Special Study Group of 15 experts to explore the following question: If we pursue a policy of disarmament and persuade the other nations to turn over control of all military forces to the United Nations so that war is no longer possible, how can the governments of the world maintain control of their people? The group concluded that war is the main control device, but alternatives such as a perceived threat from outer space, blood sports and exaggerated environmental threats might serve the purpose. Contrary to instructions, one member released the study results in 1967 under the title *Report from Iron Mountain*. (Controversy still rages today as to whether the report was legitimate or concocted)

In 1963, the CIA reached its lowest point, conducting Operation Zipper, which coordinated the efforts of the military-industrial complex to assassinate President John F. Kennedy for his work at peacemaking with the Soviet Union and in Vietnam.

In 1965, the CIA began Operation Phoenix, an intelligence-gathering program in Vietnam which resulted in the death of some 40,000 civilians.

The CIA began Operation Orwell in 1970, spying domestically on U.S. politicians, judges, law enforcement agencies and religious leaders.

In 1972, the Bank of Credit and Commerce International was formed, based in Luxemburg. It grew to having 400 branches in 78 countries and was engaged in money laundering, drug trafficking and terrorist activities for the CIA, MI-6 and Mossad. It was involved in the Banco Nazionale del Lavoro scandal, Iraqgate, Iran Contra, the looting of the Savings and Loan Associations and the Mena drug smuggling operation. It collapsed in 1991 and resulted in the indictments of a number of Americans and others.

In 1974, the Director of Central Intelligence, James Schlessinger, ordered CIA agents to compile a list of past CIA activities of questionable legality. A list of some 700 actions was assembled. It became known as the Family Jewels report.

1975 became known as the Year of Intelligence. So many of the CIA's illegal activities came to light that three committees were formed to conduct investigations. The White House formed the Rockefeller Commission, the real purpose of which was to cover up the abuses as much as possible. The House of Representatives formed the Pike Committee and the Senate the Church Committee. Senator Church was especially dedicated to the task and described the CIA as a "rogue elephant on a rampage."

Also in 1975, the CIA began Operation Condor to support right-wing military dictatorships in South America.

In 1977, the Franklin Community Credit Union Scandal came to light. The CIA was found to be involved in the kidnapping and sexual abuse of children by former high-ranking FBI agent Ted Gunderson and others. (In 1990 a grand jury concluded this was a hoax, but many credible investigators insist this was a federal whitewash, now known as "The Franklin Cover-Up.")

Also in 1977, DCI Stansfield Turner fired 800 of the CIA's 1,200 covert operations personnel, leaving only 400 experienced agents.

Congress passed the Foreign Intelligence Surveillance Act in 1978. This allowed the CIA to conduct surveillance in the United States, provided that they got approval from the court of that name.

In 1980, the CIA was involved in Operation Gold Bug, the looting of the Savings & Loan Associations and Operation Eagle Claw, an unsuccessful attempt to rescue the hostages in Iran.

October Surprise was an interesting gambit. 1980 was an election year. Ronald Reagan was running against President Jimmy Carter. The President was negotiating with the Iranians for the release of the hostages, preferably before the November elections, hoping for an October Surprise release to enhance his re-election chances. The Republicans were also negotiating with the Iranians, but for a delay in the release until after the elections. Unlike the Democrats, they offered weapons to the Iranians, who were engaged in a war with Iraq. The Republicans won the deal and with it the elections. The hostages were released on the day that Reagan was inaugurated in January. The CIA obtained the release of weapons from top secret NATO Reforger stores.

In appreciation for the CIA's efforts on his behalf, President Reagan issued Executive Order 12333, U. S. Intelligence Activities, in 1981. It allowed the CIA to spy on U. S. citizens and to conduct covert operations in the United States.

From 1982 to 1989, the CIA ran drug and weapons trafficking from Mena, Arkansas to the Contras in Nicaragua, under the protection of Governor William J. Clinton. Weapons were sent to the Contras and cocaine came to the United States.

Jonathan Pollard, a clerk in the Office of Naval Intelligence, was arrested in 1985 for spying for Israel. Vast amounts of information had been passed. Some of it found its way to the Soviet Union. Pollard was convicted in 1987 and given a life sentence.

In 1986, the Counterterrorist Center was set up as a multi-agency group in the CIA. Also in that year, the Iran-Contra scandal came to light after the shoot-down of a CIA Southern Air Transport C-123 in Nicaragua.

In 1987, the CIA began Operation New Wave. This involved bringing drugs into the United States from Southeast Asia. The

Drug Enforcement Agency, Customs Service, Department of Justice and Mossad cooperated with the CIA in this effort.

In 1991, the Nonproliferation Center was established to discourage the proliferation of weapons of mass destruction. The CIA, FBI, NSA, DIA, Customs Service and the Department of Commerce were involved in this effort.

Jews have always had a prominent place in the intelligence community. In 1994, President Clinton appointed one of them to run the CIA. John M. Deutch was a lifelong Zionist, a supporter of the Israel Lobby and a member of the Council on Foreign Relations, the Trilateral Commission and the Bilderberg group. He was a chemistry professor at MIT by profession.

In 1994, Aldrich Ames, a CIA officer serving as Chief of Soviet Counterintelligence, pleaded guilty to spying for the Soviet Union for nine years.

In 2001, Robert Hanssen, an FBI agent and counterintelligence specialist, was arrested for being a Soviet spy since 1985.

In December 2001, Pakistan's Inter Service Intelligence reported killing Osama bin Laden. The CIA still needed him as an enemy in order to justify the war in Afghanistan, so a substitute was created and shown on television, supposedly admitting that al Qaeda was responsible for the September 11 attacks.

The Intelligence Reform and Terrorism Prevention Act was passed on Dec. 17, 2004. It created a new position, Director of National Intelligence, to direct and manage the intelligence community. The Director of Central Intelligence was relieved of these duties and left to focus on the management of the CIA. The National Intelligence Council was established. The Financial Crimes Enforcement Network was expanded. The Border Patrol was authorized 10,000 additional agents. Immigration and Customs Enforcement was authorized 4,000 more investigators. Broader wiretapping, surveillance, search, arrest, detention and prosecution powers were granted to federal officials. John Negroponte became the first DNI. The intelligence community has 100,000 personnel in 16 federal agencies and a $44 billion budget.

In 2006, SWIFT (Society for Worldwide Interbank Financial Telecommunications) was created. It is run out of the CIA headquarters and overseen by the Department of the Treasury.

In May 2007, President Bush authorized black operations to support a regime change in Iran.

In recent years, the CIA has resorted to severe torture of prisoners, referred to euphemistically as "enhanced interrogation techniques" such as waterboarding, rape, sleep deprivation, beatings and many other cruelties. They use rendition, in which they kidnap suspects and fly them to black sites in remote lands for torture. Even the CIA's Inspector General has been critical of these matters, as have Human Rights Watch and the International Committee of the Red Cross. Guantanamo Bay and Abu Ghraib have become well known as abusive prisons.

In 2009, the CIA hired Blackwater Worldwide as assassination contractors. They worked against insurgents in Iraq and Afghanistan. The CIA also works with other private contractors for a variety of services.

In summary, the elite founded international espionage to protect their far-reaching investments and dealings in drugs, gold and commodities. Jewish global governance is nearly complete.

CHAPTER 31

The Police State

In accordance with Protocol #1, the Jewish elite start with the premise that most people are inherently inclined to evil and therefore must be dealt with by force and fear. As they gradually gained more and more control of the federal government of the United States, they ordered the enactment of more laws to enhance the powers of the government at the expense of personal freedom. Violating the Constitution was no longer a problem, because they controlled the legal system as well as the President and the Congress.

Jews used the principle of gradualism, tightening the screws a little at a time in order to prevent a revolution by the people. And of course their involvement was kept from the "stupid *goyim*" until they were completely enslaved. Let's review some of the major steps along the way by which Jews demolished the Constitution and Bill of Rights and took control of America.

Aldous Huxley wrote *Brave New World* in 1932. This novel predicted a world in which Big Brother would rule everyone and drugs would pacify the people. Another Fabian Socialist, George Orwell, wrote a similar book entitled *1984*, published in 1949.

The *Humanist Manifesto* was published in 1933 by John Dewey and others. It placed human beings over God and led to the corruption of American morality.

The Tavistock Institute of Human Relations was formed in England in 1947 to do research on psychological control of the masses. Later the Aspen Institute was formed in the United States for the same purpose.

On May 1, 1954, a research paper entitled *Silent Weapons for Quiet Wars* was produced. It told of many devices for controlling human thought processes to win the heart and minds of the people. May 1 is an important day for the Illuminati.

The Federal Bureau of Investigation launched its Counterintelligence Program, also known as COINTELPRO, in 1956. American citizens became the subject of widespread surveillance by the federal government. Also in 1956, the International Criminal Police Organization, INTERPOL, was formed. This served to coordinate law enforcement activities on an international scale.

The Office of Defense and Civilian Mobilization, later named the Office of Civil and Defense Mobilization, was formed in 1958. It divided the United States into ten regions.

President Kennedy issued a series of Executive Orders, 10995 to 11005, in 1962. These provided for federal control of nearly every aspect of human activity in the event of a national emergency declared by the president, overriding established laws and the Constitution. These E.O.'s were later consolidated and expanded by E.O. 11490 in 1969, 12148 in 1979 and 12656 in 1988.

The Omnibus Crime Control and Safe Streets Act of 1968 created a number of new federal laws in areas formerly left to the states and also created the Law Enforcement Assistance Administration to give the federal government more control of local peace officers. The concept of police departments providing protection to the public gradually gave way to law enforcement, protecting the government.

The Gun Control Act of 1968 was a federal attempt to disarm

and/or restrict ownership of guns by average Americans. The most difficult part of Jews gaining control of America is that the citizens are allowed to have guns and about 100 million of them do own guns. Disarming the citizens is essential to making them subjects.

The Federal Law Enforcement Training Center was set up in 1970 at Glynco, Georgia. This center provides firearms and other training to a host of other federal agencies.

The Organized Crime Control Act of 1970 created more federal crime laws and included the Racketeer Influenced and Corrupt Organizations Act (RICO). It provided for treble damages for certain crimes. Originally directed at organized crime, it has come to be used against many other unpopular groups.

The Comprehensive Drug Abuse Prevention and Control Act of 1970 expanded the drug laws and included the Controlled Substances Act of 1970. What had previously been treated as a medical problem now became the subject of widespread law enforcement. Naturally this law was not enforced against the Central Intelligence Agency, where many of its covert activities are funded by drug trafficking.

Executive Order 11647, Federal Regional Councils, was issued in 1972. It was discontinued by E.O. 12407 in 1983, when the Federal Emergency Management Agency (FEMA) was placed in charge of the ten-region system.

The Foreign Intelligence Surveillance Act of 1978 allowed federal agencies to conduct surveillance of individuals suspected of being involved in spying in the United States, provided they obtained prior approval from the Foreign Intelligence Surveillance Court. The court has allowed surveillance in more than 12,000 cases and refused it in two cases to date.

Readiness Exercise 1984, also known as Rex 84, was an exercise to test the federal government's ability to rule the country independently of the states. Operation Cable Splicer was a test of replacing state and local governments with the 10-region federal government under FEMA. Operation Garden Plot was a test of martial law to control the citizens.

The Comprehensive Crime Control Act of 1984 included the Comprehensive Forfeiture Act of 1984. No longer was it necessary to convict a person of a crime or to follow due process of law. Now the government could seize assets—real estate, cars, trucks, money, or anything else, on the mere alleged suspicion that a crime might have been committed.

The Anti-Drug Abuse Act of 1988 added to the forfeiture laws. The *Wall Street Journal* has several pages every day of things taken from the public on the strength of these laws. The monetary values involved are quite substantial.

In 1989, President George H. W. Bush set up Multi-Jurisdictional Task Forces (MJTF). These consisted of various combinations of federal, state, county and local law enforcement agencies to conduct SWAT team operations. He also set up 23 detention centers, later increased to 43, to imprison dissidents. The actual raids began in 1991 and exceeded 100 in number by the time the program was "discontinued" in 1995.

One of the best known of these was the raid on the mountain home of Randy Weaver and his family in Ruby Ridge, Idaho. A siege lasted from August 21 to September 1, 1992. Weaver's wife and son were murdered, their dog killed. One federal agent died.

Even better known was the attack on the Branch Davidian compound near Waco, Texas. After a siege lasting from February 28 to April 19, 1993, the church was burned to the ground and all the inhabitants killed.

The Brady Handgun Violence Prevention Act of 1993 put many restrictions on the purchase and use of handguns.

In 1994, the Draft Army Regulations on Civilian Inmate Labor Program was issued. These pertained to the use of the dissidents captured and placed in the FEMA detention centers and were similar to the regulations which the Nazis used in their camps during the Holocaust.

The Violent Crime Control and Law Enforcement Act of 1994 outlawed assault weapons in the hands of the public. Only our military and police forces could be allowed to have such weapons.

The Communications Assistance for Law Enforcement Act of 1994 required the nation's communications companies to provide information about customers to the federal government.

The Antiterrorism and Effective Death Penalty Act of 1996 further increased the federal government's powers. People could be held on mere suspicion of terrorist activities.

One of the insiders greatest accomplishments of all time was the terrorist attacks on New York and Washington on September 11, 2001. This was a brilliant false flag operation planned, conducted and covered up by the Zionist neo-conservatives in the second Bush administration. Al Qaeda had been involved in several prior terrorist activities, including the bombing of the embassies in Kenya and Tanzania and of the *USS Cole*, so 9-11 was blamed on them. The stupid *goyim* fell for it. This allowed the elite to attack Afghanistan, where Osama bin Laden was staying and later Iraq, though Iraq was bin Laden's enemy. It also allowed them to push many laws through Congress which increased their hold on the country.

On September 22, 2001, Congress passed the Air Transportation Safety and System Stabilization Act, which included the Victim Compensation Fund. The victims or their dependents were given generous benefits in exchange for agreeing not to sue the government or the airlines for their losses. The discovery process in civil litigation could have exposed the conspiracy.

On the same day, President Bush created the Office of Homeland Security, which later became a cabinet-level department.

On October 26, Congress passed the USA PATRIOT Act, sight unseen. This contained a number of provisions which Congress had previously rejected. Members of Congress were directed to vote for it anyway, or they would be labeled as unpatriotic.

The Aviation and Transport Security Act passed on November 19. This created to very invasive Transportation Security Administration, which subjected airline passengers to intensive screenings. This group was formed to search for weapons and explosives, but now searches for anything, including money and drugs.

In response to widespread demands for control of illegal immigration, Congress passed the Enhanced Border Security and Visa Entry Reform Act of 2002 on May 14, 2002. However, this law was indifferently enforced, because Big Business wanted a large input of aliens to provide low-cost labor. The fact that open borders allow terrorists into the country was ignored.

On Oct. 1, 2002, the U. S. Northern Command was organized, with headquarters at Peterson Air Force Base in Colorado Springs. Its mission is to plan, organize and execute homeland defense and civil support missions. In 2008, the 1st Brigade Combat Team of the 3rd Infantry Division was assigned to it as a crowd control unit known as the Consequence Management Response Force, ready to deploy in the states if ordered by the President, in case of civil unrest.

Another piece of legislation was the Homeland Security Act, which passed on Nov. 25, 2002. This created the Department of Homeland Security, a massive bureaucracy which combined 22 federal agencies into one cabinet-level department corresponding to the Interior Ministry of many Communist countries.

On November 26, Congress passed the Terrorism Risk Insurance Act. This allowed the government to sell terrorism insurance to business firms.

On May 11, 2005, Congress passed the Real ID Act of 2005, which among other things required the states to issue drivers licenses complying with the United Nations International Civil Aviation Organization's biometric format standards. This involved substantial costs to the states, estimated to be $23 billion, as well as widespread privacy concerns. The insiders were forced to delay implementation of this law.

The Detainee Treatment Act of 2005, passed on January 6, 2006, allowed for "enhanced interrogation techniques" of prisoners, a euphemism for torture. They had to make extensive use of torture, along with "renditions" which take prisoners to places where they are tortured ever more, to make them confess to crimes which they did not commit relating to 9-11.

In 2006, the Automated Targeting System for international travelers was introduced.

The Military Commissions Act of 2006 was passed on October 17, 2006. It allows prisoners to be tried by Military Commissions, rather than criminal courts, without the usual constitutional protections.

On the same day, Congress passed the National Defense Authorization Act for Fiscal Year 2007, which provides for control of the National Guard by the President, rather than by the state governors and removes Posse Comitatus, thereby allowing the use of our military forces against us.

On August 5, 2007, the Protect America Act was passed. This law extends the surveillance powers of the National Security Agency and allows for warrantless eavesdropping on telephone calls and e-mails.

The Violent Radicalization and Homegrown Terrorism Prevention Act of 2007 focuses on American dissidents who are perceived as a threat to national security. Among the groups who fit into this category are military veterans, constitutionalists, anti-war protesters, pro-lifers, evangelical Christians and supporters of third-party candidates.

Because of the widespread opposition to the Real ID Act of 2005, Congress passed the PASS ID Act (Providing for Additional Security in States Identification Act of 2009). It contains provisions similar to the 2005 act, but allows the states to keep more of the revenues and taxes related to drivers licenses and motor vehicles.

The Department of Homeland Security is very anxious to get this system of national ID cards in place. The cards are to contain the individual's social security number, drivers license number, date of birth, photograph, medical history, financial history and a variety of biomedical data. It will give them far more control of the people than the Gestapo ever had.

As a result of all these laws and executive orders, surveillance of American citizens has become very extensive. Several firms have developed radio frequency identification chips, which some call the Mark of the Beast from the Book of Revelation. The Global Positioning System allows cell phone operators to track users' locations. Roadside assistance programs, such as General Motor's OnStar, allow eavesdropping on occupants of the car. Most new cars have event data recorders. Many places use highway cameras to photograph and issue tickets to speeders. Cameras scan license plates, looking for motor vehicle tax and parking ticket deadbeats. Police set up motor vehicle checkpoints. Electronic bulletin boards ask citizens to supply the police with information.

Police have become much more aggressive. They are becoming more and more like the military, with military ranks and medals. Long gone is the neighborhood cop, armed only with a nightstick. Instead we have undercover police, SWAT teams, police dressed in black, with gloved hands, storm trooper helmets and assault rifles or shotguns.

Many cities, especially New York, have installed numerous closed circuit TV cameras. They erect barricades and metal detectors and bring vicious police dogs. Sometimes even soldiers are used as well.

Many private telecommunications companies do data mining to accumulate information on their customers and they sell this data to other firms and to the federal government.

For many years, the National Security Agency conducted illegal wiretapping in conjunction with firms such as AT&T, Verizon and Bell South, but the government granted legal immunity for this activity retroactively by the Expansion of the Foreign Intelligence Surveillance Act of 1978 in 2008.

National Security Letters are administrative subpoenas which government agencies can issue with no probable cause requirement. The recipient of the letters may not disclose their existence to the subject. Thus a doctor or other professional may be required to divulge confidential information about a patient or client to the government, but not tell the patient or client that the inquiry was made.

Passports are now embedded with RFID tags.

Prior to the 2010 census, pre-census workers with GPS locators tagged the physical address of the front door of every home in America, a project subbed out to ACORN.

In summary, Jews now have Americans where they want them. We are entirely under their control. They are now ready to make their final grab of power worldwide.

Abraham Foxman, head of the ADL

CHAPTER 32

Jewish Organizations

One of the greatest strengths of Judaism is that Jews are very well organized. There are literally thousands of Jewish organizations in the United States and elsewhere. We will look at a few of them in this chapter.

There are more than 15,000,000 Jews in the world, including nearly 6,000,000 in the United States. As is the case of other large groups, there are internal differences of opinion on religious and political matters. However, Jews take great pains to present a united front to the non-Jewish world.

Jews are particularly sensitive to anti-Semitism, whether it is directed at their religion, their race, the Zionist movement, or the state of Israel. They have a vast network of people who listen for disparaging remarks or printed words, especially from public figures. Incidents are reported to their central sources and then widely reported in the media, which they control. No politician in his right mind will dare to say anything critical of Jews.

Unless otherwise noted, the organizations mentioned in this chapter are based in New York City, which is home to nearly 3,000,000 Jews.

The Conference of Presidents of Major Jewish Organizations consists of the presidents of 52 of the largest Jewish organizations in America. It serves as a coordinating body for these groups, which between them represent the vast majority of Jews in this country.

The American Israel Public Affairs Committee (AIPAC) is a registered lobby based in Washington, D.C. It was formerly known as the American Zionist Committee for Public Affairs. It has an annual budget in excess of $50 million. It is arguably the most powerful lobby in Washington. Among other things, it invites presidential candidates to make presentations before the group. Since Jews control the majority of campaign funds, as well as the press, one can scarcely refuse the invitation. The candidate must promise absolute loyalty to Israel in order to get their backing.

The Zionist Organization of America was formed in 1897, the year of the First Zionist Conference in Basel, Switzerland. It conducts educational and informational programs for Israel and for Jewry. Currently it has about 30,000 members.

A related group is the World Zionist Organization, American Branch, which is of course part of the international group.

One of the oldest Jewish groups in America is B'nai B'rith International, meaning Sons of the Covenant, which was formed in 1843. It offers religious, cultural, civic and social programs in 51 countries. It has men's lodges, women's chapters and youth groups. Based in Washington, D.C., it has about 500,000 members and a $15 million budget.

In 1913, B'nai B'rith formed the Anti-Defamation League (ADL) to combat anti-Semitism and to secure fair treatment for all citizens through law, education and community relations. It has field offices throughout the country and a budget in excess of $40 million. Today it is a major intelligence organization.

Hadassah, the Women's Zionist Organization of America, was formed in 1912. It promotes healthcare and medical research worldwide. It has about 300,000 members and a budget of about $95 million and partners with Israel.

The National Council of Jewish Women Inc. is based in New

York and has many other locations. It has a budget of over $10 million.

The American Jewish Committee was founded in 1906 to fight anti-Semitism in Russia. Today it allegedly combats bigotry and anti-Semitism. It works to protect the rights and freedom of Jews worldwide. It publishes the *American Jewish Yearbook* and *Commentary* magazine. It has about 70,000 members and a $50 million yearly budget.

The American Jewish Congress was formed in 1918. It represents American Jews and claims it is "opposed to all forms of racism." It is committed to the security of Jews in Israel, Russia and elsewhere. It publishes *Congress Monthly* magazine.

The American Jewish Joint Distribution Committee was founded in 1914. It maintains health, welfare, assistance and social programs for needy Jews in nearly 60 countries.

The World Jewish Congress, American Section, was founded in 1936. It promotes the rights, status and interests of Jews worldwide. It represents 3,000,000 Jews in 90 countries.

The American Zionist Movement was formed in 1939. It consists of twenty member organizations.

There are three major Jewish religious organizations, each representing about 1,500,000 Jews: the Union of Orthodox Jewish Congregations of America, the United Synagogue of Conservative Judaism and the Union for Reform Judaism. In addition, there is the ultra-Orthodox Chabad Lubavitch group, based in Brooklyn, which proclaims Judaism and the Torah worldwide and has about 1,000,000 members.

The Southern Poverty Law Center, based in Montgomery, Alabama, is not an exclusively Jewish group, but it works closely with the Anti-Defamation League. It focuses on so-called "hate groups" such as the Ku Klux Klan, neo-Nazis and skinheads, as well as militia groups.

The Jewish Council for Public Affairs is the national coordinating body for the field of Jewish community relations. It consists of 13 national and 122 local Jewish communal agencies.

The United Israel Appeal raises substantial funds for Israel. $269 million was raised in 2004. The United Jewish Appeal/Federation is another major fund raiser.

The Jewish Institute for National Security Affairs (JINSA), based in Washington, D.C., was founded in 1976. Its mission is to inform the public about the need for an adequate defense budget and strategic cooperation with Israel. It has about 17,000 members.

The Jewish Defense League was formed by Rabbi Meir Kehane in 1968 as a paramilitary group opposed to anti-Semitism. It works with Mossad and the Anti-Defamation League. It has been called by the FBI "the second most active terrorist group on American soil." (Al Qaeda is listed as the first most active terrorist group on U.S. soil.)

The Jewish Defense Organization was founded in 1982 as a rival of the Jewish Defense League. Its 3,500 members are militant Jews concerned about anti-Semitism. It promotes Zionism and immigration to Israel. It promises to defend Jews. It advocates the use of violence and conducts classes in self-defense and weapons.

FLAME (Facts and Logic About the Middle East) is a San Francisco-based public misinformation group which supports Israel and promulgates information about the Middle East.

This listing is only a sampling of the many powerful organizations which promote Judaism and the state of Israel. Most Jews and many non-Jews, are aware of them and their far-reaching influence.

There are more than 15,000,000 Jews in the world, including nearly 6,000,000 in the U.S. There are internal differences of opinion on religious and political matters. However, Jews take great pains to present a united front to the non-Jewish world.

Cecil Rhodes

CHAPTER 33

International Organizations

Inasmuch as Jews have always been pursuing control of the world, they have been involved in the formation of many international organizations and they constitute a higher percentage of their membership than their numbers would indicate. We have already discussed their involvement in several international enterprises, including the Rosicrucians, Freemasons, Communism and Zionism. Now let's look at more recent developments.

Alfred Milner was the leader of a group at Oxford University in the late 19th century which was financed by the Rothschilds. Others in the group included John Ruskin, Cecil Rhodes, Albert Grey, William Stead and Arnold Toynbee. They planned to control the world, based on their superior abilities. They formed the Society of the Elect and the Society of Friends in 1891 (not to be confused with the Quakers), which became known as the Round Table group. They formed branches throughout the English-speaking world. After World War I, they formed the Institute for International Affairs. In 1920, the British branch became the Royal Institute for International Affairs. In the United States, in 1921, it became the Council on Foreign Relations. Similar groups were formed elsewhere in the British Empire. Today these groups are, in effect, the shadow governments of their respective countries. Jews constitute a sizable percentage of the membership. Another group formed in the aftermath of World War I was the League of Nations. The basic objective in all these international organizations was to reach world government in small steps, with a corresponding reduction in the sovereignty of the individual nations. Citizens would have no vote in these international bodies; instead, the world's elite would control them from behind the scenes. Fortunately, the United States Senate rejected the treaty which created the League of Nations, fearing loss of national sovereignty. The Council on Foreign Relations was formed to promote internationalism in America.

In 1930, the Bank for International Settlements was founded, supposedly for the purpose of overseeing German reparations. Actually it is a central bank for the other central banks of the world. Like them, it is privately owned and it serves the interests of the international bankers.

In July 1944, the United Nations Monetary and Financial Conference was held in Bretton Woods, New Hampshire. The United Nations itself was not formed until the following year, but this conference formed the International Bank for Reconstruction and Development, also known as the World Bank, and the International Monetary Fund. In 1945, Congress passed the implementing act and also the Export-Import Bank Act.

Also in 1945, the United Nations was created. Most of the American delegates to the convention in San Francisco were members of the Council on Foreign Relations, led by Alger Hiss, who was later found to be a Communist.

The United Nations formed the General Agreement on Tariffs and Trade in 1947. This was a major step toward international control of commerce.

The North Atlantic Treaty Organization (NATO) was formed in 1949 as a U.N. regional organization to oppose the Soviet Union during the Cold War. However, instead of dissolving after the Soviet Union dissolved in 1991, it expanded to include many of the former Soviet bloc nations.

As a step toward world government, the European Coal and Steel Community was formed in 1951. The European Economic Community (Common Market) and European Atomic Energy Community (Euratom) were formed in 1957. In 1967 came the European Communities and in 1993 the European Union. This and similar groups in America, Africa and Asia will eventually merge into the global government, if all goes according to plan.

A very secretive and powerful group first met at the Bilderberg Hotel in Oosterbeek, Netherlands on May 29 to 31, 1954. They took the name of that hotel. Among the organizers were Prince Bernhard of the Netherlands, Dr. Joseph Retinger of Poland and David Rockefeller, the New York banker who was to take a prominent position in international matters. This group meets in strict secrecy every year to plan world events and to give presidents and prime ministers their assignments for the coming year.

Also in 1954, the South East Asia Treaty Organization (SEATO) was formed as another group to oppose Communism.

In 1955, the Warsaw Pact was formed by the Soviet Union and seven eastern European nations to oppose NATO. It was dissolved in 1991.

In 1960, the Organization of Petroleum Exporting Countries (OPEC) was formed to control oil supplies and prices.

In 1961, 29 developed nations formed the Organization for Economic Cooperation and Development (OECD) to promote economic development of the poorer nations.

The Organization of African Unity (OAU) was formed by 32 African nations in 1963. This became the African Union in 2002.

The Association of Southeast Asian Nations (ASEAN) was formed in 1967 as the political adjunct of SEATO.

The Club of Rome was formed in 1968 to promote the New World Order, hoping to get it in place by the year 2000. In 1978 they developed the Global 2000 Plan, which seeks to reduce the world's population from 6 billion to 2 billion by 2050.

The World Economic Forum was formed in 1971. It meets in Davos, Switzerland every winter to plan economic policy.

In 1972, the Conference on Security and Cooperation in Europe (CSCE) was formed by NATO and Warsaw Pact countries to ease world tensions. In 1995 it was renamed the Organization for Security and Cooperation in Europe (OSCE).

The Trilateral Commission was formed in 1973 by David Rockefeller and friends. It is similar in function to the Bilderberg Group, but much less secretive. Its three parts were originally Europe, North America and Japan and has now become worldwide.

Also in 1973 the Caribbean Community and Common Market was formed.

In 1985, the Group of Seven (G-7), consisting of the seven largest nations, was formed. In 1997, Russia joined, making it the Group of Eight.

The Asia-Pacific Economic Cooperation Group was formed in 1989. In 1994, this became the Asia-Pacific Economic Cooperation Agreement (APEC).

Mexico, Canada and the United States signed the North American Free Trade Agreement in 1992. It became effective on January 1, 1994. A current proposal would expand this into the North American Union, a counterpart to the European Union. Other proposals would extend this to include Central America or even the entire Western Hemisphere.

The World Trade Organization was created in 1994, replacing the General Agreement on Tariffs and Trade.

The State of the World Forum began in 1995 and has annual meetings.

The International Criminal Court was created in 1998. As of this writing, the United States has not yet joined it.

To see all these organizations listed in one place is rather breathtaking. The Jewish goal of world government is at hand.

INTERNATIONAL ORGANIZATIONS

Inasmuch as Jews have always been pursuing control of the world, they have been involved in the formation of many international organizations.

CONCLUSION

At the Crossroad

This brings us to a major crossroad. Will we sit back and let the Jews take over the world, or will we fight to keep our liberty? First, let's see what the world will look like in a few years if we do nothing. The *Protocols* give us a clear picture of what is planned. The Jewish elite will get us involved in World War III by an attack on Iran, which will result in America and Europe fighting a nuclear war against Russia and the Muslim world. Billions of people will die, as planned in Global 2000. Israel will sit back and watch her enemies kill each other off.

After the war, the survivors will come under the absolute control of Israel. No independent nations will be permitted. There will be no United States of America or any other country, no Stars and Stripes, no Star Spangled Banner, no Constitution, nor any other relic of national sovereignty.

The only religion permitted will be Judaism. It will no longer be permissible to be a Roman Catholic, other Christian, Muslim, Buddhist, or any other faith.

Big Brother will rule the world with an iron hand and millions of spies, a high-tech police state far surpassing the worst abuses of the Soviet Union. We have already seen what happened when Jews took control of Russia in 1917. The Gaza Strip is getting a taste of their force today.

The world will run something along the lines set forth in the novels *Brave New World* by Aldous Huxley and *1984* by George

Orwell. Both authors were Fabian Socialists who knew what was being planned and set out to warn us what was coming.

On the other hand, perhaps the New World Order described above is not to your liking. If so, what are you willing to do to prevent it? You have heard it said many times that freedom isn't free and that certainly is true. There are always people around who want to control everything and everyone and we need to deal with such people from time to time.

In our National Anthem, we describe America as the land of the free and the home of the brave. My friends, if we are no longer the home of the brave, we won't be free much longer.

The globalists have finally managed to awaken the sleeping giant, which is the American public. We see tea party meetings all over the country, reminiscent of the Boston Tea Party in 1773. We the People recently concluded the third Continental Congress to take back control of our nation. Grand juries have been formed by public-minded citizens to investigate and indict government officials who have overstepped the bounds of their Constitutional authority. Citizens are buying guns and ammunition in record-breaking quantities and some of them are reviving the state militias.

You may recall certain statements in the Declaration of Independence which remain relevant today. It says in part, "We hold these truths to be self-evident, that all men are created equal, that they are endowed by their Creator with certain unalienable Rights, that among these are Life, Liberty and the pursuit of Happiness. That to secure these rights, Governments are instituted among Men, deriving their just powers from the consent of the governed. That when any Form of Government becomes destructive of these ends, it is the Right of the People to alter or to abolish it and to institute new Government." … "But when a long train of abuses and usurpations, pursuing invariably the same Object evinces a design to reduce them under absolute Despotism, it is their right, it is their *duty*, to throw off such Government" (emphasis added).

Our federal government has been under the control of the international bankers for many decades and more recently under the control of the state of Israel as well. With few exceptions, Congress is not responsive to the best interests or petitions of the American people. They have made a Faustian bargain with the Devil and have sacrificed their eternal soul for money and power today. Even the President is no more than a figurehead for the power elite behind the scenes.

In November of 2010 we had the chance to elect the entire House of Representatives and one third of the Senate. As a general rule, we would have been wise to throw out most of the incumbents, as they have proved themselves unworthy of our trust. There are exceptions, of course, men like Ron Paul and several others like him who uphold the Constitution and put America first. The end result of the 2010 November elections was a win for Republicans, who took control of the House and a strong repudiation of the socialist policies of President Barack Obama.

A good guide on this matter is *The Freedom Index: A Congressional Scorecard Based on the U. S. Constitution,* published by the John Birch Society, P. O. Box 8040, Appleton, WI 54912, telephone (800) 727-TRUE. This index is updated several times a year and grades each Senator and Representative on their votes relative to limited government, fiscal responsibility, national sovereignty and traditional foreign policy of avoiding foreign entanglements.

The takeover of our federal government has been going on for many years and cannot be reversed quickly or easily. But we better continue the efforts already under way while we still have a chance.

The very heart of the globalist agenda is based on its control of money and credit. They literally create money out of thin air and use it to buy the government, the media and many businesses. Naturally they guard this power very jealously and have killed people—even Presidents—to maintain it. Nevertheless, I believe that we should repeal the Federal Reserve Act, take over the Fed's assets and transfer its essential functions to the Treasury Department. There is no need to borrow money from this private banking cartel and to pay interest on it, when the Treasury can issue currency debt-free, as provided for in the Constitution.

The financial meltdown of 2009, which is still continuing, revealed many of the weaknesses of our financial system. Most fundamentally, we have a "funny money" system with no hard assets behind it and which the bankers manipulate for their selfish interests. Another part of the problem is the existence of financial conglomerates which are described as being "too big to fail," and thus in need of government financial support. The obvious solution is to break them into much smaller units with less monopolistic powers.

Another major aspect of the globalist agenda is to gradually transfer all powers from the sovereign nations to various international super-governments, such as the United Nations, World Trade Organization, World Bank, International Monetary Fund, NATO and so forth, all under the control of the global elite rather than of the people. All these are stepping stones to world rule by Israel. Clearly all these organizations are against the best interests of the United States and the other sovereign nations of the world. In my view, we should get out of the United Nations as soon as possible and get their spy-ridden headquarters out of the United States and then withdraw from the other groups mentioned above.

Control of the media by a handful of conglomerates controlled by the insiders is another major problem which must be addressed. We have anti-trust laws in this country; let's enforce them. Break up the media monopoly.

The international bankers seek to keep us involved in wars continuously so that the government is forced to borrow more and more from them and thus give them an ever-growing flow of interest. The Constitution gives Congress the sole authority to declare war, yet they have not declared war since 1941. Meanwhile we have been involved in more than 50 unlawful wars since then, including Korea, Vietnam, Afghanistan and two wars in Iraq.

The Department of Defense is charged with defending our nation, but does very little in that regard. Instead, it is in the service of the international bankers in an endless series of wars of aggression in foreign lands. Even the National Guard and the Coast Guard, which are intended for domestic service only, are involved overseas. It is long overdue for us to bring the troops home.

We need to change our policy toward Israel. We give them many billions of dollars a year and they use it to support a holocaust against the Palestinians. Israel has become a pariah in the world. Maybe we should stop supporting them at all.

The Central Intelligence Agency has been an embarrassment to the nation ever since it was created in 1947. The Directorate of Intelligence has failed to predict many important events and the Directorate of Operations has been involved in endless illegal operations which have made us the enemy of most of the world. It is time to disestablish that criminal organization.

The Internal Revenue Service is another organization we need to eliminate. It was created by executive order, rather than by act of Congress. Its primary duty is to enforce an unconstitutional law, namely the collection of income taxes. More than one informed expert insists the Sixteenth Amendment was not properly ratified. The real function of the IRS is to act as a collection agency for the Fed, which itself is unconstitutional.

We need to repeal NAFTA and CAFTA. These free trade laws are causing us to lose many jobs, destroying our manufacturing base and leading to massive balance of trade deficits, more than $800 billion in 2008. What we need instead is fair trade, with reasonable tariffs to protect our producers.

In the process of selling us out to the globalists, our government officials have committed many crimes, including treason, for which they should be prosecuted. We have enough evidence on them to put them in federal penitentiaries the rest of their lives.

Most important of all, we must get back to the moral and ethical principles which made our country great. For much too long, religion has been suppressed and evil promoted. Let's close with a portion of St. Paul's letter to the Galatians, Chapter 5, verses 19-21. "Now the works of the flesh are obvious: fornication, impurity, licentiousness, idolatry, sorcery, enmities, strife, jealousy, anger, quarrels, dissensions, factions, envy, drunkenness, carousing and things like these. I am warning you, as I warned you before: those who do such things will not inherit the kingdom of God."

God bless America! Down with the New World Order!

The Work of All Ages
The Ongoing Plot to Rule the World from Biblical Times to the Present

This book is a brief history of the Jewish people, from the days of Abraham to the present. The Jews are a very intelligent group, hard working and well organized, but are often resented, despised and persecuted.

From ancient times, they have had a vision of Jewish world supremacy, based on the belief that they are God's "chosen people." Today they look forward to the coming of the Jewish messiah, who will lead them to rule the world from Jerusalem. The state of Israel—in Jewish eyes the reincarnation of the legendary kingdoms of Solomon and David—however, has no problem with targeting the great Christian and Muslim centers of the world with nuclear weapons if it is threatened with destruction before this comes about, i.e., "the Samson Option."

In 33 chapters, this book reviews some of the things the Jews have done over the centuries—often in great secrecy—to advance this agenda. Included are the following: the conquest of Canaan; unity in dispersion; development of the Talmud and Kabbalah; conversion of the Khazars to Judaism; support of the Protestant reformation; development of Freemasonry; institution of central banking systems; the Rothschild Protocols; the creation of Order of the Illuminati; the creation of the Sabbatean sect—worship of Lucifer; the development of Communism and Zionism; the Protocols of the Learned Elders of Zion; the Bolshevik overthrow of the Christian czar in Russia; the creation of the Frankfurt School in Germany and the foisting of Cultural Marxism on the peoples of the Western world; control of the media; formation of the state of Israel; the infiltration and undermining of the Vatican; the globalization movement; and the institution of the so-called "New World Order."

Softcover, 230 pages, $25 minus 10% for TBR subscribers plus $5 S&H inside the United States. (Outside the U.S. add $11 S&H for one book.) Bulk discounts are available: call 202-547-5586. Order from TBR, P.O. Box 15877, Washington, D.C. 20003. Call toll free 1-877-773-9077 to charge to major credit cards. See also www.barnesreview.com. Bulk prices available: Please call 202-547-5586 to talk to a TBR representative.

In the maverick tradition of one of the great historians of the modern era . . .

No topic is "too controversial" for The BARNES REVIEW, the most interesting history magazine published anywhere today. Commemorating the trailblazing path of the towering 20th Century revisionist historian, the late Harry Elmer Barnes, TBR's mission is to separate historical truth from propaganda and to bring history into accord with the facts. Founded in 1994 by veteran American nationalist Willis A. Carto—a personal friend of Barnes—*The Barnes Review* concurs with Rousseau's maxim that "Falsification of history has done more to impede human development than any one thing known to mankind." TBR covers all aspects of history from the dawn of man to recent events and also places a special focus on the philosophy of nationalism. As such, TBR proudly describes itself as a "journal of nationalist thought" and

dares to be politically incorrect in a day when Cultural Marxism prevails in the mass media, in academia and in day-to-day life. TBR's editorial board of advisors encompasses historians, philosophers and academics from all over the face of the planet, intellectuals united in their desire to bring peace to the world by exposing the lies and prevarications of the past that have brought us to where we are today. If you believe everything you see in the "responsible" media or think that absolutely everything that appears in most college-level history texts is true, you might be shocked by what you see in TBR—but if you are shocked by what you see in TBR, then that's all the more reason you need to join the growing ranks of independent-minded freethinkers from all walks of life and all over the world who are longtime TBR subscribers.

Isn't it time you subscribe?

The Barnes Review $46 for ONE year (six bimonthly issues—64 pages each); Including this special free bonus: A FREE COPY OF Michael Collins Piper's blockbuster book *The New Jerusalem*. That's a $20 gift free for a one-year domestic subscription. Subscribe for two years at $78 and get *The New Jerusalem* PLUS Mark Glenn's *No Beauty in the Beast: Israel Without Her Mascara*. Outside the U.S. email TBRca@aol.com for international rates and for S&H to your nation.

Call 1-877-773-9077 today and charge a subscription to major credit cards.
Send your check, money order or credit card information (including expiration date) to:

The BARNES REVIEW
P.O. Box 15877
Washington, D.C. 20003

Check us out at barnesreview.org or barnesreview.com

A gutsy newspaper with some powerful enemies

A no-nonsense independent weekly alternative to the "processed news" of the corporate Media Monopoly.

The one news outlet that dares to tackle the mainstream!

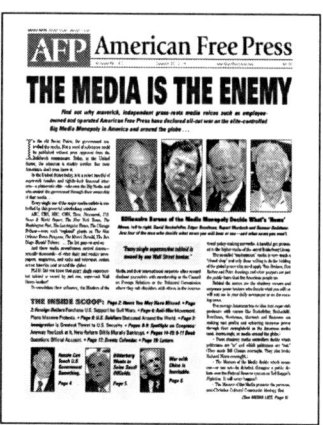

American Free Press (AFP) is the maverick national media voice that's been in the forefront reporting the uncensored news that the Controlled Media in America either ignores or suppresses.

You can count on AFP to bring the news that the major media either can not or will not report. Employee-owned-and-operated with no partisan axes to grind, AFP's reporters are committed to the truth, no matter whose ox gets gored.

AFP is the one national newspaper that's dared to tackle the Israeli lobby head on and challenge that clique of neo-conservative warmongers—that well-financed ring of arms dealers, lobbyists and "ex-Trotskyites"—who forced America into the no-win debacle in Iraq. AFP brings its readers the important stories consigned to the Orwellian Memory Hole by the self-styled "mainstream" media.

Each week—20 pages of uncensored news and information on a wide variety of topics, ranging from civil liberties and the fight against the police state to alternative health and wholistic therapies, taxes and finance, trade and foreign policy. You name it. AFP is on the cutting edge.

Big-name political figures and a host of powerful special interest groups have worked overtime to silence AFP's unswerving journalists whose track record is one that's unmatched by any other independent media voice today. If you have any doubts, why not take a look at AFP for yourself?

Isn't it time you subscribe?

American Free Press: $59 for ONE year (weekly issues) OR try out a 16-week introductory subscription for only $17.76.

**Call 1-888-699-NEWS (6397) today and charge a subscription to major credit cards.
Or send your check, money order or credit card information (including expiration date) to:**

American Free Press
645 Pennsylvania Avenue SE, Suite 100
Washington, D.C. 20003

Check us out at www.americanfreepress.net. Online subscriptions also available!

WAR CRIME HYPOCRITES EXPOSED!

THE DEVIL'S HANDIWORK
A Victim's View of 'Allied' War Crimes

CHAPTERS COVER:

- The Un-Civil War
- The Boer War
- The Dresden Massacre
- Holocaust in Russia
- FDR & His Man Friday
- Gruesome Harvest
- The Six Million Myth
- Operation Keelhaul
- Nuremberg Trials
- Katyn Forest Massacre
- Stuttgart Atrocity
- Bastardizing the Germans
- The Atom Bomb
- Cuba Betrayed
- The Invasion of Lebanon
- De-Nazification
- The Malmedy Trial
- The Dachau Trial
- The Vinnytsia Genocide
- Occupation of Germany
- FDR's Great Sedition Trial
- Trujillo's Assassination
- The Morgenthau Plan
- The Writers War Board
- Bombing Myths
- Lend-Lease
- The Truth of Auschwitz
- Pearl Harbor
- Soviet Genocide in Ukraine
- More

The Devil's Handiwork is an amazing 275-page compilation of chapters on war crimes committed by the "good guys" against the "bad guys." Many of the events covered in this book are to this day censored or twisted in mainstream history books.

Softcover, 275 pages, #529, $25 minus 10% for TBR subscribers. Add $5 S&H inside the U.S. Outside the U.S. email TBRca@aol.com for S&H to foreign destinations. Order from TBR BOOK CLUB, P.O. Box 15877, Washington, D.C. 20003. Call TBR toll free at 1-877-773-9077 to charge to Visa, MasterCard, AmEx or Discover.

ONLY BOOK OF ITS KIND IN THE WORLD!
MARCH OF THE TITANS

Here it is: the complete and comprehensive history of the White Race, spanning 500 centuries of tumultuous events from the steppes of Russia to the African continent, to Asia, the Americas and beyond. This is their inspirational story—of vast visions, empires, achievements, triumphs against staggering odds, reckless blunders, crushing defeats and stupendous struggles. Most importantly of all, revealed in this work is the one true cause of the rise and fall of the world's greatest empires—that all civilizations rise and fall according to their racial homogeneity and nothing else—a nation can survive wars, defeats, natural catastrophes, but not racial dissolution. This is a revolutionary new view of history and of the causes of the crisis facing modern Western Civilization, which will permanently change your understanding of history, race and society. Covering every continent, every White country both ancient and modern, and then stepping back to take a global view of modern racial realities, this book not only identifies the cause of the collapse of ancient civilizations, but also applies these lessons to modern Western society. The author, Arthur Kemp, spent more than 25 years traveling over four continents, doing primary research to compile this unique book—a book to pass on from generation to generation. New deluxe softcover, signature sewn, 8.25" x 11" format, 592 pages, four-page color photo section, indexed, appendices, bibliography, chapters on every conceivable White culture group and more.

High-quality softcover, 592 pages, #464, *$42*

Available from THE BARNES REVIEW, P.O.Box 15877, Washington, D.C. 20003. TBR subscribers take 10% off. Call 1-877-773-9077 toll free to charge to major credit cards. Also se www.barnesreview.org.

The Origins of Western Civilization:

A Survey of the Economic, Social & Political Forces That Have Revolutionized The Western World

Perhaps no other small book ever printed has so completely encapsulated the entire history of the Western world—and so precisely identified the root causes of its advance and decline—as has Dr. Harry Elmer Barnes' Origins of Western Civilization. Barnes was an astute student of the economic, social and political world and only he, alone among the great historians of the age—could have boiled this vast history down to its bare essentials. As you journey through this book, you will see the great cultures of the West rise and fall for reasons so simple as free trade, the quest for precious metals, usury, debt slavery and the pursuit of freedom. Along the way you will see obvious relationships to today's world where the same motivating factors and similar problems that have plagued man since the days of Egypt, Greece and Rome appear again and again as core elements in the rise and decline of nations. Barnes was born June 15, 1889 in New York state and died at his home in California on August 25, 1968. The lessons this book teaches are still as pertinent today as when he wrote it over 50 years ago. A must read for any student of history. Perfect for young and old.

THE ORIGINS OF WESTERN CIVILIZATION
Softcover, 115 pages, #510, $18 plus $3 S&H inside the U.S.
TBR subscribers may take 10% off the list price of this book.

Order from THE BARNES REVIEW, P.O. Box 15877, Washington, D.C. 20003.
Call 1-877-773-9077 toll free to charge to major credit cards.
Add $6 per book S&H outside the U.S.

TBR ORDERING COUPON TBR subscribers take 10% off book prices

Item #	Description/Title	Qty	Cost Ea.	Total
		SUBTOTAL		
		Add S&H on books*		
	Send me a 1-year subscription to TBR for $46**			
	Send me a 2-year subscription to TBR for $78**			
			TOTAL	

*S&H ON BOOKS: Add $5 S&H on orders up to $50. Add $10 S&H on orders from $50.01 to $100. Add $15 S&H on orders over $100. Outside the U.S. double these S&H charges.

TBR SUBSCRIPTION PRICES: U.S.A: $46 one year; $78 two years. **Canada/Mexico: $65 per year. **ALL OTHER NATIONS:** $80 per year delivered via air mail.

PAYMENT OPTIONS: ❏ CHECK/MO ❏ VISA ❏ MC ❏ AMEX ❏ DISCOVER

Card # _____

Expiration Date _____ Signature _____

CUSTOMER INFORMATION:

Name _____

Address _____

City/State/Zip _____

RETURN WITH PAYMENT TO: THE BARNES REVIEW, P.O. Box 15877, Washington, D.C. 20003. Call 1-877-773-9077 toll free to charge to major credit cards.

WOA411